AMAZING STORIES

FLOURISHING AND FREE

More Stories of Trailblazing Women of Vancouver Island

HALEY HEALEY

HERITAGE

For my sisters, Carmen and Alison

Heritage House Publishing Company Ltd.
heritagehouse.ca

Cataloguing information available from Library and Archives Canada
978-1-77203-353-3 (pbk)
978-1-77203-354-0 (ebook)

Edited by Nandini Thaker
Cover photograph: Edythe Hembroff and the new MG, Vancouver, Image i-66595 courtesy of the Royal BC Museum

The interior of this book was produced on 100% post-consumer recycled paper, processed chlorine free and printed with vegetable-based inks.

Heritage House gratefully acknowledges that the land on which we live and work is within the traditional territories of the Lkwungen (Esquimalt and Songhees), Malahat, Pacheedaht, Scia'new, T'Sou-ke, and W̱SÁNEĆ (Pauquachin, Tsartlip, Tsawout, Tseycum) Peoples.

We acknowledge the financial support of the Government of Canada through the Canada Book Fund (CBF) and the Canada Council for the Arts, and the Province of British Columbia through the British Columbia Arts Council and the Book Publishing Tax Credit.

25 24 23 22 21   1 2 3 4 5

Printed in Canada

Contents

Introduction
Meet More Trailblazing Women

"No country can ever truly flourish if it stifles
the potential of its women and deprives
itself of the contributions of half of its citizens."

MICHELLE OBAMA

IT CAN BE hard to follow your own path. Various forces shape
people, their actions, and their life journeys. Like the rain, wind,
and waves shaped the shorelines and land features of Vancouver
Island, various factors have consciously and subconsciously
conditioned women, both historic and current, to act in certain
ways. Society, families, traditions, individual friends, social media—
all these things exert certain pressures on people to act in certain
ways. It takes strength to challenge these influences and to flourish
despite ingrained systems. The women in this book flourished
despite hardships and setbacks, making for interesting and
remarkable life stories. Some of their life stories were innocent
and good; others had questionably immoral aspects to their lives
and careers. But they all lived life their own way. Sylvia Stark
faced racism while homesteading on Salt Spring Island, and Edith
Berkeley conducted and published research on marine worms in
a time when few women were publishing scientific papers under

Introduction

their own names. Minnie Paterson completed an epic night hike through a west coast storm to rescue sailors shipwrecked on a tempestuous shoreline known as the "Graveyard of the Pacific." Barbara Touchie created a written alphabet for the Barkley dialect of the Nuu-chah-nulth language. All of these women flourished in their own ways.

Vancouver Island has been home to many remarkable women throughout history. Some were from families who lived on Vancouver Island for thousands of years; others arrived after living elsewhere. Artists, adventurers, gardeners, leaders, and entrepreneurs all called Vancouver Island home, and all shaped its unique culture in one way or another.

During my research I noticed some things about women from history. Men were featured heavily in the literature—stories chock full of personal anecdotes, accolades, juicy information—while little or nothing was said about their wives. There was perhaps a sentence or two in lucky cases. I wondered about the reasons for this. Was it that they had less time for their own pursuits because running households, raising children, and organizing lives fell more heavily on their shoulders? Or were they doing amazing things that simply weren't recorded? Either way, I wanted to learn more and have their stories told.

I wanted to know about these women—what they loved to do, what kept them up at night, and how they spent their days. What held their interest and, if they had been alive today, what would have held their interest enough to make them forget to check their phones? What goals made up their five-year plans? What did they do for fun? But the scarce information given about these women was often only in relation to their husbands, which made me want to showcase their stories even more. They, too, must have led interesting lives. They, too, had stories worth telling. To me, discovering history encourages a sense of place, deepening our connection to places in our lives. Stories of the past can root us and afford us deeper relationships to the places we live, work, and play.

The women in this second book are no less remarkable than the women my first book, *On Their Own Terms*. Nor are they more obscure compared to the others. I learned about some of these women—including Minnie Paterson, who I discovered at a Nanaimo Historical Society presentation—after completing *On Their Own Terms*. Darn it, I thought. I forgot one! When Heritage House asked me about a second book, I saw it as the perfect opportunity to include the women I had missed featuring in the first book.

I chose women with a variety of interests and strengths. Mary Ellen Smith was passionate about politics. Edith Berkeley studied deep sea worms. And Jennie Butchart created a garden from a limestone quarry. Like the women from *On Their Own Terms*, some of the women in this book were outwardly rebellious and others more quietly confident. Stella Carroll and Pansy May Stuttard owned brothels in Victoria and Sea Otter Cove, respectively. I wanted to include these women not for their actions and behaviour but for their strength of character.

WHETHER YOU ARE a visitor to Vancouver Island or have made your home there, I hope you enjoy these women's stories. Like with *On Their Own Terms,* I opted to order the stories geographically from south to north. Read the stories in order from start to finish, or start with the one that captures your interest most. Whatever

order you proceed through the book, I hope you enjoy exploring
life as a lighthouse keeper near Victoria; I hope you revel in the
beauty of unique gardens in Qualicum Beach and Mill Bay; and I
hope you are thrilled while travelling to the west coast of Vancouver Island to see the revitalisation of the Nuu-chah-nulth language.
Stories keep us connected to the land, to each other, and to history.
I truly hope these stories add some flourish to your life.

Note of Reconciliation

THIS BOOK WAS written on the traditional and unceded territory
of the Snuneymuxw First Nation. Some of the women featured
in this book were settlers and newcomers to the area we now call
Vancouver Island, but I do not condone colonization or any of the
shameful behaviours that came with it. I have chosen to feature a
selection of women whose traits and stories sparked my interest.
I hope to convey their bravery and uniqueness by sharing their
stories. I recognize reconciliation as not a single task, but a way
of being and a way of understanding. I fully and completely support reconciliation in all its forms and recognize my own role in
reconciliation.

7

1

Mary Ann Croft
Lightkeeper

TO SAY THAT being a lightkeeper at a remote British Columbia lighthouse was a unique profession is a vast understatement. What other careers involved isolation, living at work, trimming wicks, and being responsible for the safety of hundreds of lives? Being a lightkeeper has always been much more than a job—it's a lifestyle. A way of living immersed in the weather, living intimately with the land and ocean, and often being deliciously self-sufficient. Oftentimes lightkeepers' only companions for hundreds of kilometres were the people of their household. Weather was paramount in their lives. Rain, fog, darkness, and ocean swell were constant companions. Lightkeeping life was both freeing and confining at the same time: they were free to structure their days while being simultaneously limited in where they could go.

Beyond the romantic appeal of lightkeeping, there were broad considerations to taking it on as a career. If you were on the west

Discovery Island lighthouse, where Mary Ann Croft worked.
COURTESY OF VANCOUVER MARITIME MUSEUM

coast of Vancouver Island you were protecting vessels on a part of water called the Graveyard of the Pacific. Remote lightkeepers contended with a lack of fresh food, lack of working technology, and lack of communication. In early days, lightkeepers talked about the perpetual dampness in their houses. Lighthouse stories have become lore. There are stories of chickens and cows being blown off cliffs at Triangle Island off the northern tip of Vancouver Island; of men turning on each other after being in confined quarters for too long; of a lightkeeper on Race Rocks becoming a skin diver so he could collect gold sovereigns from the ocean floor; and of lost treasure retrieved from shipwrecks far below the lighthouse.

Lightkeepers both past and present know faulty equipment, lack of sleep, lack of fresh food, weather reports, and the pressure to keep people safe on harsh coastlines. Qualifications include resourcefulness, the ability to endure hurricane-force winds like they're an everyday occurrence, and a reverence for the natural world that is bigger than a love of people and society. Physical fitness is a must, as physical jobs abound. Not to mention mental resilience in the face of loneliness, isolation, and unrelenting weather. Job risks were unique. For example, mercury was once used in the bearings of the lens mechanisms and lightkeepers would inhale mercury vapour in the beacon room. Sometimes what people saw as cabin fever was mercury poisoning. Lightkeeping was a truly no ordinary job.

Mary Ann Croft was Canada's first female lighthouse keeper. Her story is one of trailblazing, rebellion, and resilience. Though many women were involved in lightkeeping and often undertook lightkeeping duties with their husbands, Mary Ann Croft was the first woman to be solely in charge of a lighthouse. She worked during a time when shipwrecks were so common and catastrophic that the first section of the newspaper that people commonly flipped to was the marine notes or shipping news section, which listed recent shipwrecks. These frequent shipwrecks made lighthouses vital and lightkeepers heroic.

MARY ANN BRINN was born on Salt Spring Island, British Columbia, on February 10, 1865. Her parents, Sarah Ganner Brinn and Richard Brinn (a Welshman), were married in 1861 at the Methodist Church in Victoria. Along with Mary Ann, they had two other children: a daughter named Eliza, a few years younger than Mary Ann, and a son named George, who died in infancy.

On January 7, 1885, Mary Ann married a man from Ontario named William Croft, who worked as a teamster, someone who drove teams of draft animals. The wedding took place in Nanaimo at the Wallace Street Methodist Church, overlooking the ocean and harbour on present-day Front Street. Mary Ann was twenty; William was twenty-eight. Little is known about their life together, but it's thought that William died and that was when Mary Ann moved with her daughters to the Discovery Island lighthouse to help her aging father.

Lighthouses hold a rich and important place in British Columbia's history. The Discovery Island lighthouse, originally built in 1885, was one of the first on the British Columbia coast. Discovery Island is the traditional territory of the Songhees People and was named after the ship Captain George Vancouver used to explore the west coast of North America, the HMS *Discovery*. Discovery Island's lighthouse got a steam-powered foghorn in 1889. This foghorn sounded for eight seconds at a time and added an auditory warning to mariners supplementary to the visual one the lights afforded. In 1893 the fog alarm bell was replaced by a louder steam alarm plant. The Discovery Island lighthouse provided light and sound warnings to the entrance of the Haro Strait, an important shipping route between Canada and the United States.

In 1886, at the age of fifty-three, Mary Ann's father, Richard Brinn, was appointed the first lightkeeper at Discovery Island, nearly five kilometres offshore from Oak Bay, British Columbia. After her husband died, Mary Ann moved to Discovery Island with her two daughters—Edith Carmen Brinn Croft, born in 1887, and Effie Calla Brinn Croft, born in 1888. Richard was hospitalized in 1901 and died in September that year of heart disease. He was seventy-five. BC Archives records show that Mary Ann's mother, Sarah, died in 1901 as well, but give no indication of how or under what circumstances. After her father's death, while government officials searched for another lightkeeper, she was the natural replacement since she grew up at the light and knew its operations better than anyone. A letter of recommendation from family friend Harry H. Warden to Captain John Irving—manager and partner of the Canadian Pacific Navigation Company—even before Mary Ann's father died, indicated that Mary Ann did much of the lightkeeping work for years before her father died: "The greater part of the responsibility of both the light and fogwhistle has fallen upon her for years—for her father is a feeble old man and it is but a short time at best that he can live." However, she was a woman, and Canada did not permit female lightkeepers.

Women were no strangers to lighthouses. Since lighthouses had keepers, women had lived there and assisted their husbands with the daily operations despite not being compensated for their efforts. The first lighthouses on the west coast opened at Race Rocks and Fisgard Island in 1860. Historically, there were a few cases of lighthouse wives being the natural choices to take over the lightkeeper position after their husbands had died, but they were denied the opportunity because it was "against the rules of the Department [of Marine and Fisheries] to place Lighthouses in [the] charge of women."

So, it was 1901 and Discovery Island needed a lightkeeper. Mary Ann was the natural choice to take over after her father but couldn't because no woman had been a lightkeeper before. So people petitioned the federal government saying they wanted Mary Ann to be lightkeeper. In the meantime, Mary Ann was competently tending to the lights she had been helping run for years. Despite being experienced and capable, she had to fight to collect signatures to stay on as a lightkeeper. The petition worked. On April 9, 1902, Mary Ann Croft was appointed to the Discovery Island lighthouse—the very lighthouse where her father worked—and made history as the first female lightkeeper in Canada. The assistant, Henry Cumner Watts, who operated the foghorn, left that year. There was no reason indicated in historical records for his departure.

Mary Ann Croft was a diligent and skilled lightkeeper at Discovery Island light for twenty-three years. She singlehandedly ran the lights, maintained the lighthouse buildings and infrastructure, and raised her two daughters. Discovery Island and the lighthouse were her home; there was nowhere else she wanted to be.

Lightkeeping today is a job that requires physical strength and mental fortitude. Even more so in Mary Ann's time, the regular tasks at any lighthouse—which included stoking the steam fog signal, painting the station's structures, trimming wicks, and cleaning the light lens—demanded a lot from both the body and the mind. Mary Ann had the duties of raising and educating two daughters on top of these tasks—all while coping with isolation from the rest of the world. Work was never-ending. In 1908, James Gaudin, the marine agent in Victoria, reported that Mary Ann "kept the station in a highly creditable and efficient condition."

Mary Ann also found the time and energy to fight for equal compensation for her work as a lightkeeper. It came to her attention that she was earning far less than the lightkeepers at other lighthouses with foghorn alarm stations like hers. She wrote to her member of parliament in Ottawa, Ralph Smith, asking for her wage to be increased from $900 a month to $1,200 a month, making it on par with what the lightkeeper at nearby Trial Island, south of Oak Bay, was earning. She received a letter back saying she would be getting a raise and would have her pay matched to other lighthouses with foghorn alarms.

Lightkeepers are renowned for performing heroic deeds and nautical rescues. Mary Ann Croft was no different. Five years after taking over the lights on Discovery Island, Mary Ann noticed a small boat stranded on the rocky shore down the beach from her light station. She ran to investigate and found a very cold and confused older man who had been fishing with a friend in a separate boat when they became separated in thick fog. This man had been lost for three days and was nearly unconscious and hypothermic. Mary Ann wasted no time in giving him warm, dry clothes and food. He stayed at the lighthouse for two days until he recovered and returned to his home on Lopez Island, one of the nearby American San Juan Islands.

At the age of fifty-four, Mary Ann began considering retirement. She applied for a pension only to find out that lightkeeper pensions had been cancelled in 1892. She had no choice but to keep working; she would be unable to support herself if she retired without a pension. In a letter to her MP, Simon Fraser Tolmie, she wrote, "I think that after 23 years' service in such employment as the Lighthouse Branch, a person is due for some rest and something to make that rest free from worry for whatever few years that may be left." Since she could not get a pension, she worked another thirteen years and devised her own way of making some extra money to survive on in retirement: she would assist the rum-runners.

Rum-running was the illegal trafficking of alcohol, much like bootlegging, but was typically carried out over coastal waters rather than over land. Though the production, transportation, importation, and sale of alcohol was illegal by constitution in both Canada and the US—after all, these were the days of prohibition— well-organized alcohol smuggling networks existed near to Victoria and Vancouver. The most famous rum-running ship was the five-masted steamship *Malahat*, which smuggled more alcohol than any other ship on the BC coastline. Prohibition in British Columbia lasted from 1917 until 1921, while in the United States it went from 1920 until 1933. In their book, *To the Lighthouse: An Explorer's Guide to the Island Lighthouses of Southwestern BC*, John Walls and Peter Johnson discuss Mary Ann's geographic location between the American waters of Admiralty Inlet and the Strait of Georgia as a convenient location to relay messages between rum-runners. Mary Ann became aware of the trafficking networks that existed nearby and eventually became involved herself. Using the communication devices at her disposal at the lighthouse and her advantageous location, Mary Ann assisted in communications between the rum-runners operating around Victoria and Vancouver. She was well compensated and saved the money for her eventual retirement. If her employer wouldn't give her a pension, she would earn extra funds herself!

Walls and Johnson note that in 1932, thirteen years after planning to retire, Mary Ann left Discovery Island for good. At sixty-seven years old, she finally retired. She had saved enough rum-running money to rent a place in the exclusive Marine Chalet apartment building in Oak Bay. By this time, lightkeepers could once again receive pensions, so she also had a monthly pension of $43. The windows of her chalet looked out to the ever-changing ocean and Discovery Island, her home and workplace for thirty years.

MARY ANN CROFT died on April 13, 1935, at the age of seventy. She was buried at Victoria's Ross Bay Cemetery. In 1934, she received an Imperial Service Medal from the Lieutenant Governor for her devotion to duty through lightkeeping.

Of course, Discovery Island remains. In 1972, it became a marine provincial park, and 151 acres of the island are now provincially protected. It still has a lighthouse, but no lightkeeper. In 1997, the lighthouse stopped being staffed. After having faithful human lightkeepers for 110 years, its light is now operated by a computer. In 2004, the loyal foghorn was deactivated and removed.

Some intriguing mysteries surround Discovery Island and the sea that surrounds it. Cadborosaurus has hundreds of claimed sightings since the 1940s. Charmed as Canada's Loch Ness monster, tales of the thirty-foot sea creature still float around Vancouver Island today. A more recent mystery is the lone wolf that was first seen on Discovery Island in 2012 and spotted frequently after that, standing regally on rock cliffs or loping along the shore. Named Takaya, he lived for years on Discovery Island, until he swam over to Victoria in January 2020 and was captured, released, and later shot by a hunter. Discovery Island has captured peoples' imaginations. Today it's a popular boating and kayaking destination.

Some see lightkeeping as romantic: an idyllic lifestyle devoid of stresses or hardships; a life where you can do as you please. Many people think it's freeing to be devoid of exact hours and to be miles away from any bosses or supervisors. This stereotype of lightkeepers living a laid-back, paradise life is warped. A gaping hole exists between this misguided romantic notion and the reality of life on the lights. Realistically speaking, lightkeeping has complex and exceptional challenges unique to the profession. It can be lonely, isolating, physically difficult, and mentally draining. In Mary Ann Croft's day, communication was slow and by post only. There was no internet, no phones, and no other method of immediate communication. There were no stores, no hairdressers, no bakeries, no doctors, and no hospitals. A life of lightkeeping could be simultaneously freeing and confining.

Mary Ann Croft, Canada's first female lightkeeper, was a woman like no other. Unlike other women at the lights, she wasn't assisting her husband lightkeeper; she *was* the lightkeeper. This was highly unusual for a woman at that time. She fought for equal pay and raised her children while working a job that pushed people to the physical and mental limits. Nicknamed by police as the "Queen of the Rum-Runners," she would have had a huge repertoire of stories to tell.

CHAPTER

2

Victoria Chung
Physician

VICTORIA CHUNG achieved her childhood dream of becoming a doctor and medical missionary. She diligently worked toward her goals and achieved many firsts, both in British Columbia and Canada. She was the first Chinese-Canadian doctor, the first female Chinese-Canadian doctor, and first female intern at Toronto General Hospital. Her legacy remains both in Canada, where she was born and raised, and in China, where she spent most of her life working as a surgeon, hospital administrator, and medical missionary.

Victoria's story as a missionary differs from those of many other missionaries. In her time, many missionaries were male and white; Victoria was female and of Asian descent. Her story was nearly forgotten and is likely still unknown to many. While Norman Bethune, a Canadian missionary doctor from Gravenhurst, Ontario, made it into the history books and even the Canadian Medical Hall of Fame, Victoria Chung's story was not well known or documented. In fact, Victoria Chung's story may have been lost and forgotten completely had it not been for the research and writing of academics John Price and Ningping Yu, much of which is compiled in their book, *A Woman in Between: Searching for Dr. Victoria Chung*. Price and Yu recount Victoria's life starting with her childhood spent in Victoria, British Columbia, and continuing on to her life and work in China.

VICTORIA CHUNG was named after Victoria, BC (the city of her birth), and Queen Victoria, who was celebrating her diamond jubilee. Like thousands of other Chinese men, her father, Sing Noon Chung, came to Canada as a foreign worker. He arrived in Victoria in 1881 along with 15,000 other Chinese men who came to do construction work for the transcontinental railway. It was dangerous work that saw Chinese men receive only a third of the daily pay of white men. Many men died on the job.

Thankfully, Sing Noon didn't die working on the railway, and in 1885, after the railway was built, he had saved enough money to bring his wife, Yin Han, to Canada from China. He paid an additional $50 head tax that was put in place in 1885 for any Chinese people immigrating to Canada. Both Sing Noon and Yin Han were from Kongmoon, a city in southern China that's known today as Jiangmen. Upon arriving to Victoria, Yin Han worked as a midwife, using midwifery training attained in China. In her community, she was vastly outnumbered by men. By 1891, men made up 95 percent of the Chinese residents of Victoria.

In 1897, Sing Noon and Yin Han had their first daughter, who they named Victoria. The couple would have three more children. When Victoria was five or six years old and ready to attend school,

Victoria Chung.
COURTESY OF UNITED CHURCH OF CANADA ARCHIVES

her parents enrolled her in kindergarten in the Chinese Rescue Home, later renamed the Oriental Home. This home was operated by the Woman's Missionary Society of the United Church and fulfilled many functions: it was a school, a boarding school, a women's shelter, a foster home, a respite home, and a hospital. Even weddings were held there on occasion, and the Presbyterian and Methodist Churches also did missionary work through the building. Victoria's parents shared a strong Christian faith.

The Oriental Home was a big part of Victoria's life. She boarded there for a few years of her childhood while her other siblings were young, and in the process, gained something vital for her life journey: education. The Victoria School Board banned Chinese students from attending their schools in 1903, so Victoria attended the Oriental Home for school until 1909, when Chinese children were finally permitted to attend public school in Victoria. The Home also gave Victoria a platform to fight against racism and for gender equality, and would later assist her with a scholarship to attend medical school.

The woman Victoria saw the city she was named after assume some major changes. In her childhood, it was a new Hudson's Bay Company fort. Within her lifetime it would transform from a small trading fort to a much larger bustling city centre. It was also a racially divided city. During Victoria Chung's childhood, Chinese people were not treated well, and many lived in Victoria's Chinatown.

Chinatown in Victoria was the first one to be established in Canada and the second in North America—San Francisco's being the first. Chinatown was usually composed of a few streets of close-knit communities. In Victoria, this started as a few three-storey brick buildings with back alleyways and passages but later grew in geography and population. By 1861, Victoria's Chinatown was a single block where present-day Douglas, Fisgard, Store, and Pandora Streets exist. A narrow backstreet connecting Pandora and Fisgard Streets was nicknamed Fan Tan Alley, after a game of chance called "Fan Tan" that was popular in the late 1800s.

Though Victoria's Chinatown started as a collection of theatres, shanties, cabins, tailors, gambling parlours, and opium dens, it soon grew to have barbers, butchers, cafes, grocers, and herbalists. Market gardeners sold vegetables and fruit, while peddlers sold clothes, fabrics, and sewing supplies. The professions of people living in Chinatown fell into two main categories: workers and merchants. Victoria Chung's father started out as the former and transitioned into a career as the latter. By the late 1890s, tourists walked Chinatown's streets, and Chinese New Year was celebrated in Victoria by all residents. Victoria's Chinatown had a population of 3,000 people during the ten years before and after the turn of the twentieth century.

Racism was rampant in the city of Victoria during Victoria Chung's childhood. In 1884, the province passed laws that disallowed Chinese people from owning crown land and forced them to pay extra annual taxes. Schools were racially segregated with separate schools established for Asian students. Some businesses refused to hire Chinese employees, and Chinese people were banned from voting and working on public works projects.

Victoria Chung's schooling began with attending the Oriental Home and then transitioned to the public school once Chinese students were permitted to attend public schools. As a young girl, Victoria expressed wanting to be a medical missionary in China. The first step toward this goal was reached when, after graduating from Victoria High School in 1916, she was awarded a scholarship from the Presbyterian Missionary Society. She applied to and was accepted at the University of Toronto. It was the only medical school in Canada that allowed female students at the time she applied. Although female students were allowed, they endured harassment, sexist chanting from students, and sexist remarks from even their professors. In 1922, Victoria Chung graduated from medical school and became an intern at Toronto General Hospital—the first woman to be an intern there. In 1923, she wrote her final exams and prepared to go overseas to work as a missionary. The Women's Missionary Society appointed her to the Marion Barclay Hospital for Women and Children as part of the

Victoria Chung

United Church's South China Mission. Victoria had reached her goal: she was about to become a missionary doctor in China.

In 1923 something else also happened. The Chinese Immigration Act, better known as the Chinese Exclusion Act, was passed and halted Chinese immigration to Canada. Victoria's parents decided to move back to China and join Victoria there. The Chinese population in Victoria, British Columbia, decreased drastically after the Chinese Exclusion Act was passed.

The Marion Barclay Hospital for Women and Children was in Kongmoon, the Chung family's hometown. It was funded mostly by the Woman's Missionary Society in Montreal but received funding from various missionaries in Canada. Now known as Doctor Chung, Victoria was a competent and highly valued addition to the hospital. She was a skilled surgeon and was also appointed the hospital administrator, managing the entire hospital. On top of these major duties, she also taught nursing and worked in the hospital's medical dispensary. She accomplished great things for the hospital and the region. Under her direction, the hospital expanded from thirty-three beds to more than two hundred beds. In 1923, her work brought an ambulance to that area of rural southern China, as well as modern hospital equipment, modern medical practices, and medical supplies.

Victoria left China every five or six years, usually to visit family and friends in Canada and to attend furloughs—leaves of absences to attain more training. She left in 1929 and took a year's leave. She visited family and friends in Canada and undertook more training. As a lifelong learner, Victoria was determined to continue progressing and excelling as a doctor. Between 1936 and 1937, she went to England for three months to train at the London School of Hygiene & Tropical Medicines. She also undertook graduate training at Bellevue Hospital in New York City, and spent another leave of absence studying in Toronto. During these periods, she would sometimes give presentations.

The first half of the twentieth century was a tumultuous time in Chinese history, with many rebellions and revolutions, including the Chinese Civil War, and the establishment of many military dictatorships that began in 1925. It was also in 1925 that Victoria's hospital was shut down due to resistance among Chinese people to foreign enterprises, which the hospital was considered to be since its funding came from Canada. Eventually, it was able to reopen, and Victoria returned to work. When the Japanese Imperial Army launched a full-scale invasion of China in 1937, Victoria could have gone back to Canada; she was a Canadian citizen, after all. But she didn't—she stayed at the Marion Barclay Hospital and continued to manage it, caring for refugees and the wounded when Kongmoon was bombed. By 1939, many of the other Canadian missionary doctors had left, but Victoria was still running the hospital and even keeping a vegetable garden to feed staff and patients. One likely reason Victoria did not return to Canada was that the Chinese Exclusion Act would have prevented her mother from returning to Canada with her. Mostly, though, her life's work was at the Marion Barclay Hospital for Women and Children, so that's where she remained.

Back the Marion Barclay Hospital, Victoria cared for refugees, both at the hospital and in an outreach capacity. She vaccinated against smallpox, typhus, and cholera, and treated for dysentery and malaria. Victoria never gave up on her patients, even if their conditions seemed hopeless. She lived in a residence behind the hospital which she shared with her friend Dr. Annie Wong and her mother.

Ultimately, in 1941, Victoria's beloved Marion Barclay Hospital for Women and Children was taken over by the Japanese. John Price and Ningping Yu explain how a Japanese guard came and took the hospital keys off Victoria and forced her and other missionaries to leave. Missionary doctors were considered enemy aliens and not to be trusted. Victoria continued to remain in Kongmoon, where she and two graduate nurses ran a small hospital and dispensary during the eight years of the Second Sino-Japanese War—she would not leave her mother, her friend Dr. Annie Wong, her cousin, or her patients. Together, they served the poor and anyone needing medical assistance. Eventually, in 1945, the Second World War ended and Japan, defeated, withdrew from China. Victoria, her mother, Dr. Annie Wong, and her cousin moved back to their residence behind the Marion Barclay Hospital, and eventually, Canadian missionaries also returned to China to work there.

When she was fifty-eight years old, Victoria adopted a twelve-year-old son named Songqia. He moved in and lived with Victoria, Dr. Annie Wong, Victoria's mom, and Victoria's cousin, who was a pharmacist. In her later years, Victoria brought her medical expertise to remote areas of China that lacked medical care. She truly cared about people—whether they resided in city apartments or countryside cottages.

VICTORIA CHUNG died of lung cancer on May 17, 1966. Hundreds of people stood in the streets of Kongmoon to honour the woman who had given herself to her missionary work. Across the Pacific Ocean, in the city of her birth, Victoria Chung's death was mentioned in the United Church files in Victoria, British Columbia.

Victoria is remembered as being a doctor who was professional, skilled, hard working, and constantly improving. An article in the *Peterborough Examiner* describes Victoria's achievements as a medical missionary: "In five years this efficient Canadian-born woman broke all records for out-patients, in-patients, and confinement cases in her hospital." Largely due to Victoria Chung's work, the Marion Barclay Hospital for Women and Children was known for delivering top quality medical care. She somehow found time to write for the *China Medical Missionary Journal* published in Shanghai. Victoria never forgot the help she had to attend medical school. She repaid all the money she had received from the Presbyterian Missionary for her medical training at the University of Toronto. This money was used to establish a Dr. Victoria Chung scholarship fund to help deserving students to pay for their education.

Victoria left a legacy for her competence and strength as a leader, having brought new equipment like telephones, electricity, x-ray machines, and typewriters to the Marion Barclay Hospital. She was credited for running a well-equipped, well-led, and modern women's hospital. She constantly fought for the same resources for the women's hospital that existed at the men's hospital.

Despite all her work and achievements, Victoria's story might have been forgotten. How had Norman Bethune, another Canadian surgeon, been deemed a hero and become known across Canada while Victoria Chung had not? She only became known after she had died. After her death, Victoria Chung was honoured on two continents. In 2012, Jiangmen Central Hospital put up a bronze statue of Victoria Chung that stands in the reception area. The Chinese government named her a national hero of culture. In the same year, the City of Victoria declared December 8 Dr. Victoria Chung Day.

Victoria Chung was a true trailblazer. She let nothing get in the way of her goal of becoming a missionary doctor. She worked as a missionary doctor in China for forty-three years and through tumultuous political times always remained deeply committed to her patients and hospital.

Today we might use a fancy word like "intersectionality" to describe Victoria Chung and the overlapping discrimination she faced for being a woman and a person of colour. But she lived her life, strived to reach her goals, and worked hard to transform her dreams into reality. Did she feel a rush of excitement after reaching her goal? Did she savour that delicious feeling of having accomplished what started out as a mere idea?

Victoria lived life her way, forging new paths and crushing her goals. She adapted through challenging political times, at one time telling the *Toronto Star* that "one must take things as they come." She lived her personal life her own way, choosing an unconventional family structure over a traditional one. She lived with her friend and adopted a son. She was many firsts, including first person of Chinese descent—man or woman—to graduate from a medical school in Canada. Victoria Chung is remembered as a medical hero and was certainly a trailblazing woman of Victoria, BC, the city she was named after.

CHAPTER

3

Amelia
Connolly Douglas
Métis Pioneer

AMELIA DOUGLAS'S BRAVERY and quick thinking saved her husband James Douglas from murder. Shortly after their marriage, Amelia and James were living in Fort St. James, a Hudson's Bay Company fort in northern British Columbia near modern-day Vanderhoof. Relationships were tense between the HBC and the Dakelh People. Earlier that year, James entered a house belonging to Chief Kw'eh, a great Chief of the Dakelh People of Nak'azdli Whut'en, and killed a man. The Chief's nephew hunted down James Douglas to retaliate and grabbed him. When Amelia arrived on the scene, the Chief's nephew had a knife to her husband's throat, ready to kill him for entering his house and for murdering the man. Amelia thought quickly and made a plan. She decided to throw as many valuable goods as she had at the man trying to kill her husband. She knew that giving trade goods was a sign of respect in some Indigenous communities and hoped that doing so in this situation would appease the Dakelh People. So, she and an HBC interpreter tossed tobacco, clothing, food, and as many other goods as they could at the man holding the knife to her husband's throat. Then they waited and hoped for the best. The man removed the knife from her husband's throat and accepted the gifts they had tossed toward him. Her plan worked. Though several versions of this story exist, a common thread is that Amelia's cultural knowledge and quick thinking and action saved her husband's life.

Thanks to a split-second decision on Amelia Douglas's part, James Douglas lived to continue to make a significant mark (whether good or bad) on what would later become the province of British Columbia. Had Douglas been killed, perhaps the course of west coast colonial history would have been altered in some way. How differently would the history of the province have unravelled if Amelia had not saved James Douglas's life during this interaction? Though she was not quite as well known as her husband, Amelia Douglas led a noteworthy life.

AMELIA DOUGLAS was born on January 1, 1812, deep in Canada's wild boreal forest near Thompson, Manitoba—a settlement more than 700 kilometres north of Winnipeg. This landscape was untouched, wilderness dotted with lakes and traced with snake-like meandering rivers that looped through tall and spindly black spruce forests. Her mother, Miyo Nipiy, was the daughter of a Swampy Cree Chief from Rat River, a Hudson's Bay post south of Winnipeg. Her father, William Connolly, was fur trader of

Lady Amelia Douglas.
IMAGE M09894 COURTESY OF CITY OF VICTORIA ARCHIVES

French-Canadian and Irish descent from Lachine, Quebec. She also had an older brother nine years older than her.

Children born to fur traders, or voyageurs, and Indigenous women back in the 1800s were called various names depending on who was referring to them. Voyageurs called them "Métis," Cree people called them "mixed-bloods," and the British derogatorily called referred to them as "half breeds." The Cree word for these people was "ápihtawikosán." Amelia's mother spoke Swampy Cree; her father spoke French. Amelia became fluent in both and did not learn to speak English until later in her life.

John Adams wrote much about Amelia's life in his book, *Old Square Toes and His Lady: The Life of James and Amelia Douglas.*

He discusses how Amelia's father's work as a fur-trade voyageur took the family all over what is now Canada. William Connolly worked closely with Indigenous trappers to trade furs and eventually became a chief trader of the North West Company—a rival company to the powerful Hudson's Bay Company. When the two companies merged in 1821 Amelia was nine years old, and her family moved from the river and lake country of Cumberland House in central Saskatchewan to Lesser Slave Lake in what is now northwestern Alberta. Back then, a move of this distance meant a seven-week-long canoe trip along rivers. A year later, the family moved again to Fort Fraser in northern British Columbia.

In Fort Fraser, Amelia's father got to know a co-worker named James Douglas. Douglas had joined the fur trade in 1819 and was working as a clerk for the Hudson's Bay Company. Amelia's father wanted James to stay in Fort St. James and broke Amelia's supposed arranged betrothal to another man. Amelia and James were married with Amelia's dad as officiant on April 27, 1828. She was sixteen and he was twenty-four. James would work his way up the ranks of the Hudson's Bay Company, beginning as a clerk, making alphabetical inventory lists of products, and working his way up to Chief Trader, a position that put him in charge of an individual post. Finally, James became Chief Factor, heading districts and working closely with HBC governors. In 1858, James became governor of the Crown Colony of Vancouver Island.

James Douglas likely chose Amelia for his wife partially for love but also partially for strategy. Amelia, being the daughter of a fur trader, was competent in wilderness survival. She had spent her lifetime moving often, travelling through the wilderness, and living in isolated HBC posts. She also had knowledge of a range of local languages, cultures, and wild foods. Some HBC men married women who could act as cultural interpreters with Indigenous groups, as Amelia did when she saved James's life by offering gifts to the Dakelh people to appease their anger at him.

During the first years of their marriage, James was often away fishing or collecting furs. Eventually, Amelia and James moved to Fort Vancouver after the governor of HBC, George Simpson, posted James there. In Fort Vancouver, Amelia spent her time horseback riding, berry picking, pressing wildflowers, picnicking in the countryside, attending dances, and walking in gardens. Unfortunately, she experienced racial and social discrimination during her time there. It was in Fort Vancouver that Amelia met her best friend, Marguerite McLoughlin, the wife of another chief factor for the HBC. Marguerite was forty-six years old, but despite the age difference, they became close. John Adams notes that both women had Indigenous mothers and French fathers, and interestingly, both rode astride when horse riding while most other women rode side-saddle. Amelia had other female friends, some of whom were Indigenous women from the nearby Songhees Nation.

Throughout Amelia's life, she was faced with many struggles and much upheaval, including the loss of several babies shortly after their births. She finally gave birth to twin girls in 1834, whom she named Cecelia and Maria. Unfortunately, Maria did not survive, but Celia did, and the Douglas family grew to three. In 1837, Amelia and James were married again in Fort Vancouver, this time with a Christian service, and later had another child, named Agnes. Amelia couldn't read or write, but she told Cree stories and sang Cree legends, which she remembered from her mother, to the children. She taught her children beadwork she learned as a girl, along with sewing and embroidery. Amelia had also never stopped speaking her mother tongue, so her daughters learned to speak Cree in addition to English and French. French was the language she spoke with her husband.

While Amelia was building her new family in Fort Vancouver, her birth family back in eastern Canada was falling apart. After Amelia's parents had moved back to Quebec, her father decided to leave her mother to marry his much younger cousin. When he died, her father left nothing to Amelia's mother or siblings; all of it went to his second wife. Amelia would have been in her early twenties at this time. Amelia's mother and her youngest sister, who was just ten years old, came to live in Fort Vancouver before the family moved once again.

During this time, James was climbing the ranks in the HBC and Amelia was often left alone with the children. In 1842, James travelled to Vancouver Island to decide the location for a new HBC fort. This wilderness of trees, fog, and pebble beaches would be called Fort Victoria. Construction of the new fort began in 1843, and in 1849, Amelia, James, and the children moved there by way of a steamship called *Cadboro*. Amelia had two more daughters, named Alice and Rebecca, both before moving to Fort Victoria. The move from Fort Vancouver to Fort Victoria was difficult for Amelia. It was a move from an established fort to a remote outpost and took much getting used to. Unfortunately, Amelia's daughter Rebecca, died of illness shortly after the move in 1849. In 1851 Amelia had another baby, who she named James William, and in 1852, Amelia's oldest daughter, Cecilia, married HBC doctor John Sebastian Helmcken, who played a major role in bringing British Columbia into Confederation and helped establish the

British Columbia Medical Association. Meanwhile, James Douglas became the governor of the Colony of Vancouver Island in 1851, and then the governor of British Columbia in 1858. In 1864 Amelia became Lady Amelia Douglas when James's title was changed to Sir James Douglas. With James's quickly rising career, everyone suddenly knew Amelia Connolly Douglas. Despite this, Amelia preferred gardening and smaller social gatherings to larger crowds and continued to live a quiet life.

Amelia spent her life helping and serving the public. She learned traditional Cree midwifery practices from her mother and delivered many babies in Fort Victoria. She nursed the sick, too, and lived through outbreaks of typhus, smallpox, and measles. She picked garden produces, preserved fruit from her garden, and made jellies and jams. She gave fruit and vegetables she grew to others. Could it be that Amelia had a deep connection to the land and its earthly treasures? Amelia helped wherever she could. She was a skilled midwife and, despite her comfortable and even prestigious position in society, she didn't see herself as being better than anyone else.

ON JANUARY 8, 1890, Amelia Douglas died. She was seventy-eight years old, and like her husband James Douglas, who had died three years earlier in 1877, she was buried in Victoria, her home for forty years. As the wife of a man who had such a meteoric career in the HBC and the early provincial government, Amelia enjoyed wealth and a life of privilege. Although she had to move often and lived in wilderness outposts, she also had servants to do cooking and housework—a luxury not had by many women in her day and one that afforded her more free time than many.

Despite this, though, Amelia's life was far from easy. She lived in a time when infant mortality rates were high, having lost five of her ten children before they reached adulthood. She raised children in a world devoid of hospitals and public healthcare, and lived through rampaging epidemics. Her husband was often kept away from home for long periods because of his work, and her family of origin split up in her adult years. In addition to these hardships, she lived in a world where people were narrow-minded and held bigoted views, and as a result, she suffered discrimination for her mixed ancestry. Despite having moved her home so many times and living a colonial life, she held tightly onto her Cree culture and remained proud of who she was. She pushed on through hard times. Her Indigenous heritage seemed to be a crucial part of her identity and something important enough to teach to her children.

What might Amelia have said about her own life? Although there is some writing about her, we have no personal accounts written *by* her. Did she unearth happiness between her struggles and grief? Perhaps she found contentment in passing traditional teachings and knowledge on to her children, teaching them sewing, embroidery, and beadwork, or sharing the Cree stories and songs she'd learned from her own mother while curled up in front of a crackling fire. Her female friendships, too, seem to have been a source of happiness.

Amelia Douglas was married to one of the most prominent, though greatly disliked, men in British Columbian history. His story, as the "Father of British Columbia," largely overshadowed hers. Despite this, though, Amelia lived an incredibly rich and interesting life, forging her own path as a woman and an Indigenous person.

CHAPTER

4

Edythe
Hembroff-Schleicher
Painter and Writer

IF YOU WERE asked to think of Emily Carr, you might picture her solo: an artist painting by herself in a sun-dappled forest, solitary but for her easel and tall, moss-draped trees, and her trailer, dogs, and monkey keeping her company nearby. But no other people.

Fans of Emily Carr may know the photograph portraying her outside her trailer in a forest with her dogs and her monkey, Woo. Many more may know the somewhat iconic portrait painting of Emily in a red coat, holding her dog against a backdrop of trees. But who was with her to capture those moments? Emily had a dear female friend who was also an artist and an interesting individual. This friend painted with Emily both in studio and in the quiet forest where Emily so loved to be, and she was the person who took the trailer photograph and painted the famous portrait. Her name was Edythe Hembroff-Schleicher.

EDYTHE HEMBROFF was born in Moose Jaw, Saskatchewan, in 1906. When she was six years old, she and her family moved to Victoria, where her parents worked as merchants. Her childhood was spent near Craigdarroch Castle. Edythe attended Victoria High School and then studied art at the California School of Fine Arts in San Francisco, the California School of Arts and Crafts, and the École des Beaux-Arts in Paris, France. She also studied at Andre Lhote's studio in France. Along with attending art school, she travelled and took French lessons. Several photographs at the BC Archives show Edythe with her friend Marian Allardt, sketching in Venice and around France, and travelling around California. Solo photos of Edythe show her wearing a beret in Paris and picnicking in a park Rome, a bottle of wine in hand.

Edythe was briefly married in France, but the relationship didn't last and she returned to Canada in 1930. In 1942 Edythe married a math professor named Frederick Brand, who taught at the University of British Columbia and was a squadron leader in the RCAF. One photo from the BC Archives shows Edythe and Fred on the shoreline of a lake at Riding Mountain, Manitoba— Edythe sits elegantly on the bow of a canoe pulled up on shore and Fred stands beside her out of the water and in uniform. Another shows them on the front of a boat, looking contented and standing so close they're touching. The couple promoted Emily Carr's art together, and Fred also painted. During the Second World War, Edythe and Fred moved to Ottawa, Ontario, where they both

Edythe Hembroff-Schleicher and her first sculpture
at the California School of Fine Arts.
IMAGE I-66588 COURTESY OF ROYAL BC MUSEUM AND ARCHIVES

worked as civil servants. Edythe had a job as a translator with
the German Prisoner of War Censorship Section under the Department of Nation War Services. She took a break from painting while
in Ottawa. In 1949, Edythe and Fred divorced. Edythe's third and
last marriage was to her supervisor, Julius Schleicher.

38

It was in 1930, after Edythe moved to Victoria from France, that she met Emily Carr. Edythe was freshly returned from art school in Paris and was twenty-three years old; Emily was fifty-eight. Emily had read an article in a local paper about a painting Edythe had done on a dress and was intrigued. She invited Edythe for tea at her house in James Bay, which was a boarding house at the time. The women were kindred spirits and became fast friends. From then on, they spent time together painting in studio and outdoors.

After moving back to Victoria in the 1960s, Edythe painted, photographed, and wrote about Emily Carr. Edythe lived at 360 Dallas Road, where many of her letters were addressed from. She apparently owned the first MG sports car in Canada, and she and Emily would pile brushes, canvases, and easels into it to go painting. One BC Archives photograph shows Edythe in her new MG-T two-seater sports car (produced between 1936 and 1955), one hand proudly on the steering wheel, the other draped casually over the door. Another photo shows her driving her car in Victoria in 1941, and yet another shows Edythe smiling widely at Cordova Beach in 1932.

In the winter of 1930–31, Edythe worked in Emily's studio a few times a week. "Emily painted so many of the sketches and canvases on display in my presence, both in the field and in her studio," she wrote. Edythe also noted in a letter that she and her first husband, Fred Brand, mounted some of Emily's paintings for an art exhibit. A few of Edythe's own most famous paintings are of Emily Carr, one being a portrait of Emily with her Griffon dog, painted in 1971. Another, titled *Mr. Woo Waiting for Tea*, was painted in 1934 next to a camp stove. And yet another portrait shows Emily standing in the doorway of her trailer, named Elephant, and Edythe standing on the ground beside the trailer's door, hands clasped neatly in front of her. Two dogs and the monkey Woo stand by the women's feet; the forest forms a green background.

Edythe and Emily were similar in many ways. Both shared love of painting, both received their art education in San Francisco and Paris, and both shared a desire to be understood and respected for their art. One way they differed was age; Edythe was thirty-five years younger than Emily. The women also differed in the subjects they painted. Edythe preferred human subjects, while Emily couldn't get enough of painting trees and landscapes. The two women encouraged each other artistically and supported each other's work. Edythe encouraged Emily to switch from her beloved subject and draw something other than trees. Emily persuaded Edythe to paint in the forest, though Edythe preferred the studio. Emily also convinced Edythe to submit her work to an art show in Seattle, where she went on to win awards.

Like Emily, Edythe was also a writer. She wrote books. And she wrote many letters. She wrote letters after rejections came back from where she had submitted her writing. When her application to the Canada Council of the Arts for funding to research Emily's life in San Francisco, Britain, and France was rejected, she wrote a letter. And she wrote to people who portrayed Emily Carr in a way that was incorrect or not to her liking. In 1971, Edythe wrote a letter to the CBC expressing her disappointment in the musical production, *The Wonder of It All*, which was based on the life of Emily Carr. She also wrote letters to call out and correct errors and omissions in presentations about Emily. She wanted a perfect portrayal of Emily Carr.

A couple things inspired Edythe to write about her friend: a grant she received combined with a deep sense of obligation to provide an accurate depiction of Emily Carr for public interest. It was crucial for Edythe to portray her friend as a warm, friendly woman with a good sense of humour. Edythe felt she was the only one to do it.

Edythe wrote about her and Emily's trips to Goldstream Park—a river and waterfall rainforest paradise outside the city of Victoria, where the "trees themselves are just as she painted them." She also wrote about the development of Metchosin and Esquimalt, areas outside of Victoria that were growing and continue to spread in size to this day: "Gigantic cedars now spring from an asphalt floor instead of one of moss." And, of course, she wrote about Emily, "at the height of her creative power and her output was astonishing." She wrote of their similarities and their differences. "I flourished in the studio atmosphere where Emily wilted, and I became irritated with outdoor conditions, flimsy easel, bugs in paint, rapidly changing light and curious bystanders—which Emily somehow overlooked or overcame."

Edythe claimed only she truly knew Emily. She was defensive of people who wrote about Emily without knowing her personally. "I am the only person to ever live and work with her," she claimed in a letter to the Canada Council of the Arts. She was upset by what she called, "sensationalist literature" that portrayed Emily as an "eccentric old lady." In Edythe's view, Emily was just a normal person from Victoria, and the clothes that some people found odd were gardening and backyard clothes that Emily made herself. Edythe claimed that Emily usually wore very normal clothes.

Edythe desperately wanted Emily portrayed in the best way and as a regular person. Edythe said Emily was, "struggling against [the] atmosphere" of a narrow-minded view of art at that time and that "she was a delightful companion. I didn't find her eccentric." She got even more enraged at people who said she painted well but added "for a woman" after it.

Edythe dedicated her life to Emily Carr. At the age of seventy-three, she said, "I follow in Emily's footsteps wherever she went." Edythe went all the way to Skagway and Sitka, Alaska, where Emily had gone on painting trips. In a letter in 1973 Edythe noted that she had been involved with Emily Carr for forty-three years. In 1969 Edythe published the first book-length work about Emily, titled *M.E.: A Portrayal of Emily Carr*. In 1971, Edythe was appointed by the provincial government to be British Columbia's special consultant on Emily Carr. With this came a grant to continue her research on her late friend, which involved settling informational discrepancies and occasionally dating paintings. Her second book, *Emily Carr: The Untold Story*, was published in 1978. It took her six years to write it. Edythe's books were deemed the definitive books on Emily Carr. People were deeply curious about Emily Carr and were intrigued by works from someone who knew her personally.

Even after retiring from the special consultant position in 1982, Edythe continued fact-checking and correcting mistakes in written works about Emily Carr. She was truly dedicated to teaching people about her friend and ensuring she was portrayed in a good way, and she was adamant that she was the best person to represent Emily because of their close friendship. In her opinion, most people didn't *know* Emily, and she worried that after she died, nobody would be there to correct the dates of paintings: "I sat beside Emily while she painted literally hundreds of them."

EDYTHE DIED IN Victoria in 1994 at the age of eighty-seven. She had three unique careers, having been a painter and photographer, a civil servant, and a researcher and writer. An artist in her own right, her own work was deeply influenced by her friend Emily Carr. Her artistic mediums varied; she did much more than just paint. Photographs showed Edythe with a camera and a young Edythe with short dark hair and a closed-mouth smile behind a sculpture while at the California School of Fine Art. She took photographs of Emily Carr and her caravan in 1936 and 1938, as well as what might be the last known photograph of Emily in 1939.

The University of Victoria offers the Edythe Hembroff-Schleicher Scholarship to pre-medical female undergraduate or graduate students. Her name lives on through this scholarship as well through the numerous works of art and writing she left behind, including her paintings. Only two paintings of Emily Carr were ever done and Edythe painted one of these. That painting now lives in a permanent collection of the Vancouver Art Gallery. They are everlasting reminders of one progressive British Columbia artist painted by another artist who was also a dear friend.

5

Isabella Mainville Ross
First Female Landowner in British Columbia

MANY PEOPLE IN Victoria and on Vancouver Island know of Ross Bay Cemetery, but fewer people know the woman who once farmed on the land where the cemetery now sits. This woman was Isabella Mainville Ross, and she was the first female registered landowner in what is now British Columbia.

Like Amelia Douglas, Isabella was a Métis woman who was born far from Victoria, farther east in what was then known as Upper Canada, and who married a Hudson's Bay Company employee. In fact, Amelia and Isabella were friends and met when they both lived in Fort Vancouver. With her land, she farmed and raised her children as a strong and determined single mother.

Isabella Mainville Ross

ISABELLA MAINVILLE was born on January 10, 1808. She was likely born near modern-day Fort Frances, Ontario, close to a fur-trading outpost called Fort Lac La Pluie, which belonged to the North West Company and later the Hudson's Bay Company. Her mother, Josette Mainville, was Ojibwa and her father, Joseph Mainville, was of French and Spanish ancestry.

May Wong writes about Isabella in her book *City in Colour: Rediscovered Stories of Victoria's Multicultural Past.* In 1822, Isabella married a Scotsman named Charles George Ross, who was a boatman for the Hudson's Bay Company. The couple got married in Fort Lac La Pluie, Ontario. In her book, Wong describes the couple's moves around Canada: They moved from Fort Frances to Fort Vancouver and to Fort McLoughlin—a fur trade outpost on Campbell Island near modern-day Bella Bella on British Columbia's central coast. In Fort McLoughlin, when Isabella was trading on behalf of her husband, as she sometimes did when he was away, a man pulled a knife on her son. Isabella grabbed a knife of her own, charged at the man with it, and chased him out of the fort.

Isabella's final move with her family was to Fort Victoria in 1843. Her husband Charles received a promotion that made him Chief Trader for the Hudson's Bay Company and he was now in charge of supervising the construction of Fort Victoria. He wouldn't see the construction to completion, however, because he died suddenly of appendicitis in 1844. This left Isabella widowed at thirty-six years old, with nine children of varying ages, including a newborn, a toddler, and three children under ten years old. Isabella and her children moved to Fort Nisqually in the Puget Sound area of modern-day Washington State, where they lived for eight years. The family eventually moved back to Victoria and, with money left

Isabella Mainville Ross.

to her in Charles's will, she purchased ninety-nine acres of land in Victoria. This acquisition was significant and historic for several reasons. The purchase of land under Isabella's name made her the first female landowner in what is now British Columbia. It also likely made her the first Indigenous person in what now is British Columbia, either man or woman, to own land under colonial rules. The year was 1854.

Isabella named her new property Fowl Bay Farm for all the waterfowl in the area. The name was seemingly a play on Foul Bay, the body of water named by Captain George Vancouver in the 1790s for its poor ship anchorage. The land Isabella purchased includes the eastern two thirds of modern-day Ross Bay Cemetery, Harling Point Chinese Cemetery, and Hollywood Park. The entire area would later be renamed Foul Bay, the spelling changed from her initial name of Fowl Bay.

Isabella's children—both the girls and the boys—attended school while she worked the land. She sold livestock and produce grown on her farm, including potatoes, which author Cecil Clark wrote about in an article in *The Victorian* on February 23, 1977: "Prior to the gold rush, she [Isabella] grew potatoes for Fort Victoria, bulk of which were peddled to the Russians at Sitka for furs."

In 1863, Isabella got married a second time, to a man named Lucius Simon O'Brien. She left him after a year. It turned out he had married her for her money and land. He slandered Isabella and her children in a Victoria newspaper after she broke off the relationship and then proceeded to leave town.

Though Isabella couldn't read or write English, she spoke French, Ojibway, and likely Chinook Jargon, a grammatically simplified language used for trade. Retired UBC professor of linguistics Jay Powell and Sam Sullivan (former Vancouver mayor) point out that Chinook Jargon, or Chinook Wawa, resembled French, English, and Nuu-chah-nulth, and that Lower Chinook was used extensively for trade from northern California to central British Columbia in the 1800s and early 1900s.

ISABELLA SPENT the later years of her life in the care of the nuns at St. Ann's Academy in Victoria. On April 23, 1885, she died at the age of seventy-seven. A tall, handsome headstone bears Isabella's name in Ross Bay Cemetery, on the very land where she used to grow potatoes and raise livestock.

Ross is a well-known pioneer name in Victoria. Ross Bay itself and Ross Bay Cemetery are both named after Métis pioneer Isabella Mainville Ross. She was the first woman to own land on Vancouver Island, and was a mother to nine children, all of whom lived to be adults—an unusual occurrence in days of high infant mortality rates and rampant disease. Some of her decedents apparently still lived near Ross Bay until the 1920s. Isabella was a prominent pioneer woman of Victoria whose name will remain in the city where she lived her pioneer life.

CHAPTER

6

Stella Carroll
Property Owner and Madam

STELLA CARROLL HAD a bold personality packed with grit. Her life was punctuated by soaring highs and rock-bottom lows. Fame and wealth were balanced by deception and heartbreak. She had financial successes and failed marriages, successful business endeavours, and police raids. After every setback, she came back stronger than before. As a participant of the controversial but historically and economically significant sex trade in bustling historical Victoria, BC, Stella Carroll was many things: an entrepreneur, sister, landlord, property owner, and upscale brothel owner—known as a madam back then.

STELLA CARROLL was born in Missouri in 1872 and had a trying childhood. Linda J. Eversole chronicles Stella Carroll's life in her book *Stella: Unrepentant Madam*, offering a detailed look at Stella's colourful life. Some of the childhood information about Stella is from this book. When Stella was fourteen years old, her mother died and Stella stepped into a mother role for her younger sister, Minnie, and younger brother, Roy. Their life was one of poverty, living in a sod house that leaked when it rained. Their father was an alcoholic.

Eventually, Stella's family went to Oklahoma for free land. Eversole describes the feverish fight to claim land that was being given away: Stella and Minnie selected a section of land, hammered wooden stakes on the edges of it, and laid out a wagon sheet. Then they sat down. Where they sat would be where they built their house.

Education was held in high regard by Stella. She ensured her siblings became educated, spending whatever it cost and paying for it with money made from her properties or brothels. Her brother went to a private boarding school in San Jose, California, and her sister went to Santa Clara, California, to attend a convent school to be trained as a teacher.

At twenty-five, in 1897, Stella moved to San Francisco. By this time, she already owned properties in Arizona and New Mexico. She had been married and divorced twice. During a previous visit in San Francisco, Stella bought a brothel from a friend after the woman originally planning to buy it died mysteriously, found at the bottom of some stairs after a wild night. This purchase started Stella's adventurous and tumultuous career owning and operating brothels—the start of her life as a madam.

In 1899, Stella moved to Victoria, British Columbia, which was a quickly growing city. Some brothel history is worth a mention as it pertains to Stella's story. In the late 1800s, the sex trade in Victoria was booming. University of Victoria scholar Patrick A. Dunae called Victoria "one of the largest sexual emporiums in the

Stella Carroll's Rockwood Estate in Victoria.
IMAGE M05694 COURTESY OF CITY OF VICTORIA ARCHIVES

Pacific Northwest." Victoria of the 1800s was certainly a different world than the "City of Gardens," as it is sometimes called today.

Victoria was founded in 1843 as a Hudson's Bay Company fort. In 1862, it had grown into a city and was part of the Cariboo Gold Rush, and by the 1870s, brothels were common, starting at the Fisgard Chinatown area and eventually moving to the Broad Street business district in later years. Thousands of people came through Victoria to the Fraser River Gold Rush, and men outnumbered women by many. The sex trade was thriving, and sexual commerce was a big part of the local economy. Prostitution started in dance houses, filled with raucous fiddle music and illegally sold liquor. Many brothel owners were women. Business ventures for women were scarce, and owning brothels, though considered to be very immoral and often dangerous, was a career some women entered for the promise of hefty profits.

There were two levels of brothels in Victoria. In one academic paper about Victoria's sex trade, Lacey Hansen-Brett explains that Victoria's lower-scale red-light district was located on Chatham and Harold Streets, while the upper-scale brothels were on Broughton, Courtney, and Douglas Streets. Stella's brothels were certainly upper-scale ones that catered to the elite and were decorated with the most lavish furniture and décor and often offered live music.

Stella operated brothels in three locations in Victoria. The first was on two rented floors of the Duck's Block building on Broad Street. Then, she bought her own property and ran the second brothel on Herald Street, and eventually bought a waterfront mansion called Rockwood on Gorge Road for the third establishment. This last location offered a more concealed place to do business, but police raids were still frequent.

Owning a brothel was a risk. In Stella's days, the brothel owner made money from the rent that the girls paid, while the girls kept all the money from their services. The owner also profited from the sale of food and liquor. Keepers of "houses of ill fame" could be prosecuted under either the federal Criminal Code or under the city's public moral bylaws. Lacey Hansen-Brett points out that, according to the Victoria City Police charge books, the men who frequented brothels were more likely to be charged than the women themselves. Fines were oftentimes dismissed, and if they weren't, they were usually between twenty-five and fifty dollars. For the owners of brothels, however, it was a different story completely. In 1892, owning and running a brothel could land you in jail for a year. Fines could be as much as seventy-five to a hundred dollars. The police and brothel owners had an unofficial quasi-business agreement between themselves. The police couldn't collect business licence fees, so they raided the brothels twice a year. The hundred-dollar fine acted as a somewhat informal business licence, and were a significant source of income for city governments.

Community attitudes toward brothels and their owners, however, were icy. Residents frequently complained to Victoria City Police about brothels, their patrons, and their owners. Moral reform groups, including the Purity League, the Local Council of Women, and the Salvation Army, did everything they could to shut down brothels, wanting to get as many women as possible out of prostitution. Many groups launched petitions against prostitution, including the Local Council of Women, which were largely ignored by the city because they benefited financially from the fines.

Legal battles were plentiful. Stella often appeared in court after being caught selling liquor without a licence. She nearly went to jail in New Westminster and Victoria, but was spared only because of a police general who didn't believe in jail sentences for madams or prostitutes. Stella was also frequently charged for operating a disorderly house. Moral reformers and neighbours regularly paraded outside her house. During one memorable raid, Eversole reports, Stella was caught selling liquor to soldiers in uniform and for operating a brothel too close to a military encampment. In response to the charge, Stella reportedly stated: "The military were evidently in dire need of saving from the likes of a sick, one-legged, 46-year-old woman." She seemed to keep a light spirit even in the most stressful of circumstances.

One night, Stella was injured in a mysterious accident. She was found at Rockwood with a gunshot wound in her leg, her husband at the time beside her. It appeared they were using chloroform as a recreational drug and Peter had shot her. Stella had to have one of her legs amputated and Peter was found to be not at fault. He said he accidentally shot the gun while trying to unload it. Peter and Stella broke it off shortly after this accident and he left town. Eversole describes Stella as shrewd, clear-headed, but also quick to temper. There are stories of Stella flying into a full rage when police raids happened at her brothel. She was said to be very jealous of her sister anytime she was around her husbands.

In her glory, Stella owned a parlour house on Gorge Road called Rockwood. In *Stella: Unrepentant Madam*, Eversole describes Rockwood as a spotlessly clean, regal space, complete with oriental rugs, leather armchairs, velvet drapes, and a piano. The house itself was good looking and well kept.

When Victoria landlord Simeon Duck died in 1905, and brothels were starting to close (or go underground), Stella left Victoria and moved back to San Francisco. Eversole describes Stella's last business endeavour as a boarding house for shipyard men working near San Francisco. By this time, Stella had a wooden leg and was living with chronic gall bladder pain. She got married one last time, this time for love, to a man named Martin Fabian. Twelve years after being married, he died of a heart attack while working in construction on the San Francisco Bay Bridge.

Despite her career and personal losses, Stella found joy in her later years. According to Eversole, Stella lived out her retirement in a small town called Alameda, near San Francisco. Her last days were spent in a cottage in Lake County, California. Joy was her dogs and driving her nieces to see the giant redwoods. She apparently loved fairs, parades, travelling, and dressing fancily in lace dresses. Stella loved animals, too, and at one time had five small white dogs.

Her temper was balanced by the light-hearted side of her personality. Stella died in 1946 and was buried in a Los Angeles cemetery. The inscription on her headstone reads, "Estella Carroll Fabian: Beloved sister."

STELLA'S NAME still lingers around Victoria history circles. In 2018, the *Times Colonist* wrote about the current state of the Duck's Block Building, the location of Stella's second Victoria brothel. Located at 1316 Broad Street, the building has been standing since 1892. Now owned by the University of Victoria, it was turned into condominiums for graduate students. The top two floors of the five-storey building were Stella's from 1899 to 1907.

Stella achieved her goals and prevailed over adversity. At the height of her career, she owned a successful, high-class, upscale brothel in what is now the Gorge area in Victoria, BC. At her lowest, she dodged prison sentences, but she lived her life hard, never giving up or backing down from what she wanted. She never lost sight of her dreams and never stopped pursuing her goals. Stella lived a life of entrepreneurism: In a time when brothels, although technically illegal, were a part of the social and economic realities of many west coast cities, including Victoria, she took advantage of those realities when she decided to work as a madam. Regardless of the moral value of her career, Stella kept going no matter what hardships she endured. She stood her ground, never quit, and, above all, had a zest for life.

7

Josette Legacé Work
Métis Pioneer

JOSETTE LEGACÉ WORK was a Métis woman and wife of a Hudson's Bay Company voyageur. She lived the life of a fur-trading voyageur and travelled with her husband on many trapping and trading trips. These trips were no leisurely canoe journeys. Mornings were brutally early, often starting before the sun rose. Days were incredibly long. Rivers were flowing roads used to travel great distances to deliver and trade furs carried in bundles packed in the canoes. When the rapids were too dangerous to paddle, the voyageurs got out of the canoes and carried their canoes and bundles of fur around the rapids—often two bundles at a time, each bundle weighing ninety pounds. After brutal days of paddling and portaging great distances, canoes and gear were repaired. Voyageurs often slept under canoes; trips could last for months on end. Life was physically and mentally tough.

Josette Legacé Work.
IMAGE A-01826 COURTESY OF ROYAL BC MUSEUM AND ARCHIVES

Voyageurs were major players in the history of Canada. Many of these voyageurs were Métis people, the descendants of European and Indigenous Peoples. Métis people suffered discrimination from both European and Indigenous people for being of "mixed" ancestry. It was an isolating existence for some. Josette Legacé Work lived this physically and mentally tough life as the wife of an HBC voyageur. She spent the settled part of her life in Victoria, BC, where she is remembered as a prominent Métis pioneer.

JOSETTE LEGACÉ was born in 1809 near Kettle Falls, Washington. Her mother, Emma Legacé, was a Spokane Indigenous woman and her father, Pierre Legacé, was a Métis voyageur of French and Indigenous parentage, whose job as a voyageur was to transport furs through the wilderness by canoe and on foot when the rapids were too dangerous to paddle. Fort Colville, near Kettle Falls, was Josette's home until she got married in 1826. She married John Work (a name anglicized from Wark), who left Donegal, Ireland, at the age of twenty-two to work as a trader and trapper for the Hudson's Bay Company. When Josette married him, John was the Hudson's Bay Company officer constructing Fort Colville. He would later move up the ranks in the company, eventually becoming Chief Factor.

These marriages between HBC men and women from areas near the fort were called "à la façon du pays," or "in the custom of the country." They were married by a minister in November 1849 at Fort Victoria. Hudson's Bay Company men considered it a great advantage to marry a woman of Indigenous or mixed European and Indigenous background, since these women were used to living in the wilderness, could travel easily with their husbands, and were able to create and maintain relationships with other Indigenous Peoples whose territories they travelled through.

While Josette and John lived in Fort Colville, John embarked on trading expeditions, sometimes alone and sometimes with Josette. She accompanied him to eastern Washington, Montana, and as far south as California. She was pregnant for some of these expeditions and had their first daughter while on a trip, on land that is present day Idaho. Josette and John moved to Fort

Vancouver (current-day Vancouver, Washington). There, Josette met two women who would become lifetime friends: Amelia Connolly Douglas and Marguerite McLoughlin.

In 1836 Josette moved to Fort Simpson (today known as Lax Kw'alaams) near Prince Rupert, BC. Here, Josette spoke out against slavery, which was affecting some of the northern Indigenous Peoples. She also apparently took up taxidermy, stuffing birds to preserve them. Josette and John lived at Fort Simpson for twelve years. Two of their daughters stayed in Fort Vancouver for schooling and later moved to Oregon to continue their education, but they also sought more educational opportunities for the rest of their children. For the years they lived in Fort Simpson, the Work children had been homeschooled, and a desire for more robust educational opportunities for them spurred Josette and John's next move.

In 1849, the family moved to Fort Victoria, where there were schools and churches. Josette and John were married a second time, this time in a religious ceremony, by an Anglican minister in November that year. Then in 1852, Josette and John purchased a large amount of land from the Hudson's Bay Company—523 acres, to be exact—at the going price of a dollar an acre, according to the Victoria Heritage Foundation. The land they purchased was on today's Hillside-Quadra area, near Topaz Park and the present-day border between the City of Victoria and Saanich. They had a log cabin built and would later build a mansion for the family. Their property was called the Hillside Farm, and they often hosted riding parties, high tea, and dinner parties there. In addition to this land, Josette and John bought property at Gordon Head and Mount Tolmie. This brought their total owned land to about eight hundred acres and made them owners of the most property in the Colony of Vancouver Island.

In Victoria, Josette nurtured her friendships with other wives of HBC employees, including Amelia Connolly Douglas, who she knew from Fort Vancouver, and Isabella Mainville Ross. (See Chapters 3 and 5.) Josette and John had twelve children together—most were born in Fort Simpson, but one was born on their travels in what is now Idaho and another was born in Victoria. Josette's eight daughters were young women during the Fraser River Gold Rush of 1858. At this time, suitors started stopping by the Hillside farm to court the girls, and when each got married, Josette and John gave them a lot of land and a house. Three married very prominent men whose names live on today in Victoria: the eldest, Jane, married Dr. William Fraser Tolmie, an HBC official who was also a surgeon, scientist, and politician (their son, Simon Fraser Tolmie, served as premier of British Columbia between 1928 and 1932); their second daughter, Sarah, married Roderick Finlayson, a HBC chief factor and politician; and one of their younger daughters, Mary, married James Allan Grahame, who became a HBC chief commissioner. Josette remained close with Amelia Connolly Douglas for her entire time in Fort Victoria. In 1861, John died and Josette became a widow. She continued to live in Victoria, becoming a prominent matriarch and outliving John by thirty-five years.

JOSETTE LEGACÉ Work died on January 30, 1896, in Victoria. In her later years, she preferred being called Suzette Work, and signed her name as such. That is the name that appears on her large, monolithic headstone in Victoria's Ross Bay Cemetery. After her death, the BC legislature paid Josette tribute for her work as a pioneer who had done many good deeds. She and John had been well loved members of the Victorian community.

Josette lived a fur-trading life and became a well-respected pioneer of Victoria. She witnessed Victoria grow immensely, transforming from a rugged frontier town to a sophisticated city. She was a prominent Métis woman, and together with her children and grandchildren, held much political and economic power on Vancouver Island.

CHAPTER

8

Jennie Butchart
Gardener

THE BUTCHART GARDENS viewed from above is like an artist's pallette. Splotches of canary yellow daffodils, clusters of orange and red tulips, and large carpets of thick green grass, nourished from winter showers. Bubble-gum-pink cherry blossom petals rain from cherry trees that line a curving driveway. Magnolia blossoms send a light sweet fragrance floating through the air, lavish in their continuous spout of sugary scent. Pathways like grey rivers twist through flower beds, and paths of stepping stones cross rippling blue ponds. California redwood trees reach higher than anything else in the garden, rooted in soil but striving for the sky. Rhododendrons boast colourful bunches of magenta, their smooth green leaves reflecting the sunlight back into the sky. Tiny dots of people meander through the splotches of colour, stopping to capture the garden with cameras or smartphones. Happy voices

Jennie Butchart

Jennie Butchart.
IMAGE M00552 COURTESY OF CITY OF VICTORIA ARCHIVES

and easygoing laughter hang in the air. When the talking subsides, water fountains and birdsong fills the space.

The Butchart Gardens is a cheery place created by an interesting woman for an even more intriguing reason. Jennie Butchart was the artist gardener who dreamed up and created the world-famous gardens off Tod Inlet at the southern end of Vancouver Island.

JENNIE BUTCHART was born as Jeanette Foster Kennedy in Toronto, Ontario, on February 26, 1866. Author Dave Preston describes Jennie's childhood in his book, *The Story of Butchart Gardens*: her mother, Martha Kennedy, was of Irish descent but born in Canada, and her father, James Kennedy, was an Irishman who worked in Ontario as a commission merchant dealing hay, straw, and seed. Jennie's father died the year she was born, so Jennie lived with her mother near Lake Ontario in Toronto until she, too, died when Jennie was twelve. After that, Jennie moved to Owen Sound, a few hours' drive northwest of Toronto, where she lived with her aunt and seven cousins.

Young Jennie was energetic, athletic, and loved trying new things. As a small girl, she learned to drive a four-in-hand, a carriage pulled by four horses and driven by one person. She ice-skated, rode horses bareback, and tried hot air ballooning. She once told a reporter that she "rode [horses] almost as soon as [she] could walk." In his book, Preston said Jennie rounded up cattle with her large collie, much to the dismay of her aunt, who thought it unladylike. She apparently also flew in a plane with Louis Blériot, the French pilot who first flew over the English Channel. Rumours alleged she even took control of the plane during the flight.

Jennie was intelligent, artistically talented, and attended Brantford Young Ladies' College. She graduated in 1885 with top marks and true talent for painting and academics. She planned to marry a stable owner so she could always be around horses, but after graduation, she met someone who was totally different. Robert Pim Butchart, the Scottish son of a hardware store owner, was a rising star in the cement industry. Robert's keen business sense and cement ambitions would take him and Jennie far, literally and fiscally.

Jennie and Robert got married in Buffalo, New York, in 1884. She was eighteen; he was twenty-seven. They honeymooned in Europe and while there, Robert secured a special cement recipe from a long-lost English relative in Canterbury. Upon returning to Canada, Robert established the Owen Sound Portland Cement Mill near Owen Sound, Ontario. While living in Ontario, Jennie and Robert had two daughters named Mary and Jenny (purposely spelled differently). Robert's success in the cement industry made him known as the "father of the Canadian cement industry."

In 1902 Jennie and her family moved to Victoria, British Columbia, as Robert set his sights on new cement business opportunities in the west. At first, Jennie was painfully homesick and desperate to return to her friends, family, and everything else she knew and loved in Ontario, but eventually, she came to love the landscape and forest of her new west coast home. A few years after moving to Victoria, Jennie and the family moved twenty-one kilometres north of Victoria to a property on Tod Inlet, which extended off the eastern side of the Saanich Inlet.

The Saanich Peninsula is a thirty-three-kilometre-long headland located twenty-one kilometres northeast of Victoria. It is home to gnarled Garry Oak forests, red arbutus trees that only grow near oceans, and massive Western red cedar trees, and is inlaid with lakes and ponds. Its protected location in a rain shadow means that it enjoys warm and dry growing conditions. Nowadays, the Saanich Peninsula is home to many farms and wineries and is nicknamed the "Provence" of Vancouver Island.

Jennie and Robert, however, didn't move to the Saanich Peninsula for the beauty above the ground. They moved there for what lay beneath. Among various types of bedrock below the Saanich Peninsula lay rich limestone deposits. And limestone was used to make cement. Jennie and Robert opened a cement plant, calling it Vancouver Portland Cement Company. Jennie worked as a chemist in the cement plant's laboratory, employing the chemistry certificate she earned at school back in Ontario. The first cement sacks from Vancouver Portland Cement Company left aboard the ship *Alexander* in 1905. Jennie and Robert were progressive in the cement industry for putting cement from their plant in sacks rather than barrels.

The cement plant was hugely successful. Cement was in high demand in the early 1900s. West coast cities like San Francisco and Seattle were growing, and this booming construction meant that cement was needed in large amounts. Jennie and Robert valued the local economy and the Vancouver Portland Cement Company prioritized cement supply for local builders and engineers over international ones. By 1909 the Vancouver Portland Cement Company's quarry was dug out of limestone. There was nothing left to mine, and what remained was a gaping hole in the earth where the limestone had been taken from. Filled with tired and rusty equipment and rock walls, it was a 3.5-acre-wide eyesore, barren and without life. Their house looked onto this unsightly view; Jennie was not happy. One day she decided to do something about it. Jennie described inspiration coming to her "like a flame, the limestone pit burst into imaginary bloom." So she said to Robert, "Let's plant it with flowers, Bob. Let's make it beautiful." Jennie had always been artistically talented, intelligent, and motivated—turning the cement pit into gardens was a perfect project.

Jennie set out to make her vision a reality. Trouble was, she didn't know the first thing about gardening—but she was determined to learn. And she had the bonus of having financial means to hire help. She called botanists. She read many gardening books. Robert hired his cement workers to help her. And she hired Japanese landscape architect Isaburo Kishida to landscape the garden. Jennie was determined to make her garden dream come true.

First, she had to attain soil. She used topsoil from the Saanich Peninsula, and had it brought in by the ton using a horse and buggy. Then for plants and flowers. She started simply, by planting roses and sweet peas around their house. Then, she planted some flowers beside the stream that sloped down to Tod Inlet. From there she planted pansies, petunias, marigolds, and violets. Many of the flowers were planted from seeds that she attained from friends or from her and Robert's expansive travels, which they did each year between the wet, dark, and rainy west coast months of January and March. One unique addition to her garden were Tibetan blue poppies, which have cyan blue petals and lively yellow stamens. Jennie secured plants and flowers from Yukon, Alaska, the Himalayas, and the Pyrenees. For Jennie, the rarer and more unusual the plant, the better.

Her garden grew. And grew. And grew some more until what was once a limestone quarry became a garden of epic proportions. The garden overflowed with blooms and had several distinct sections. The former quarry pit itself was named the sunken garden, accessed by descending fifty feet of switch-backing staircases. Plants covered its entirety, including its rock walls. To plant ivy high on the quarry's walls, Jennie suspended herself from a rope using a bosun's chair, a sort of harness with either a wood plank or canvas seat often used to clean the windows of tall buildings or in rock climbing. Suspended fifteen metres in the air above the sunken garden, Jennie carefully planted ivy in every available space on garden's stone walls. Along with the sunken garden, there was a Japanese garden, a rose garden, an Italian garden, and a Mediterranean garden. An observation platform overlooked the sunken garden, transformed from a tower used when it was a quarry. Poplars hid the old cement factory building.

Jennie collected seeds and flowers for her gardens wherever she went. She collected flowers from friends who lived locally. She brought seeds from trips she and Robert took after Christmas until spring. Physical structures from their travels adorned their gardens: fountains, sculptures, and ornaments. Eventually Jennie's quarry-turned-garden held alpine flowers from Tibet, like the blue poppies, and according to one urban legend, one of the cherry blossom trees in the garden came from the Emperor of Japan. Robert bought ducks, peacocks and pigeons for the gardens. A concrete smokestack is a reminder of the garden's unique industrial history and its transformation from an old quarry to being hailed as one of the "five great private gardens of the world." Its reclamation from an industrial site was unusual for that time and quite innovative, demonstrating Jennie's forward-thinking creativity.

By 1921 Jennie's sunken garden was complete. She named the gardens and property Benvenuto, meaning "welcome" in Italian. It was a fitting name, considering Jennie's abundant hospitality to all. Wanting no profit from her creation, she simply wanted people to enjoy her gardens. She was known as "a woman of great warmth and charm who put everyone at ease in her presence and had a quick and refreshing sense of humor," and she had an astute emotional intelligence that let her fit in with anyone and in any social situation.

Word spread in Victoria about the gardens on the outskirts of the city. Visitors began arriving. It began with guests who had received invitations, but even uninvited guests were welcomed.

Jennie didn't charge admission, saying she wanted the flowers to be, "free for all." In 1915 alone, Jennie served tea to 18,000 people, and King George VI and Queen Elizabeth visited the gardens in 1939. Jennie opened her gardens to visitors seven days a week.

Jennie apparently dressed simply, frequently sporting a cotton dress, straw hat, and gumboots. On other days she wore overalls and carried a trowel. She wore no jewellery and, after losing two wedding rings, decided not to get a third. In a time when many wealthy women would have hired people to maintain their gardens, Jennie did not sit idle and watch others work on hers; she got her hands dirty—no chores were below her. Before beginning her project, Jennie knew nothing about gardening, but by the end it, she was being asked to judge horticulture competitions in Canada and the United States.

Jennie frequently struck up conversations with garden guests, even befriending some of them. She picked bouquets for guests, made them cups of tea, or showed them her personal favourite flowers. She was casual and at home in her garden, and didn't mind if guests picked a flower from the many blooms. And she refused to post any KEEP OFF THE GRASS signs. Guests would sometimes mistake Jennie as garden staff; she wouldn't correct them, keeping her identity as owner of the garden concealed as she gave them a cheerful tour around the property. She would then politely refuse any tips offered to her. She also gave away fruit from the garden to local hospitals.

Jennie rolled with the punches and kept the garden growing through some challenging times. During the Second Word War, she just barely managed to keep the gardens going, keeping on the minimum number of workers to operate. Once, during the war, Jennie invited soldiers from Work Point Barracks for tea. She was expecting 600 soldiers; to her surprise, 1,200 showed up. She didn't miss a beat, cutting the prepared cakes in half and jovially welcoming all 1,200 soldiers. In 1939 Jennie and Robert apparently tried selling the gardens for only a dollar. The upkeep deterred any potential buyers, including the Province of British Columbia, the Municipality of Saanich, and the City of Victoria. So, after the war, out of necessity to keep it running, Jennie and Robert began charging twenty-five cents per person to enter the garden.

Eventually, Jennie took a step back from her beloved garden, but kept it in the family. In 1939 she gifted it to her grandson Ian Ross as a twenty-first birthday present. As a former lawyer and Royal Navy officer in the Second World War, Ian wasn't a gardener. But he, like his grandmother did years earlier, took on the challenge of the garden. He hired gardeners, maintained it, and even installed the Ross fountain. Furthermore, he brought symphony concerts to the gardens for music lovers and puppet shows for the children. He also continued to operate the tearoom. Ian is remembered as working very hard to keep the garden going. Like his grandmother, physical work was not below him and he could sometimes be seen carrying chairs away from the puppet house after a show or bent down yanking weeds from the garden beds. He, too, remained anonymous when mistaken as staff by garden guests.

In 1941, Jennie and Robert moved out of their house at The Butchart Gardens and into Victoria. Robert died in 1943 at ninety-six years old. Like his wife, he had been a well-loved citizen of the Victoria area.

JENNIE BUTCHART died at her home in Victoria on December 12, 1950. She was eighty-two years old. It was said that she commented on the beauty of the sunset just moments before passing. She had a simple service, devoid of flowers. This was her request before she died. Her ashes were scattered over the blue waters of Tod Inlet, where Robert's ashes had been scattered and next to the gardens she had so intensely loved. And the gardens? They had already been transferred to her grandson Ian Ross years before, and he would safely keep them growing, passing them down in later years to his son, Christopher. In 1977 Christopher brought weekly firework shows to the garden. Each person in the Butchart family brought their own flair to the property.

Jennie Butchart loved people, and the people of Victoria loved her. She was remembered as being welcoming to all, gregarious and a great conversationalist. Major Cuthbert Holmes, an occasional dinner guest and President of Pemberton Holmes Ltd., said of Jennie: "Talking to Jennie Butchart was like conversing with a master of a great university. She was at home on any subject, asked pithy questions, and went straight to the heart of any topic under discussion." She also loved storytelling and practical jokes. In her later years, she would sit in her window and watch people enjoy her gardens. She was voted Victoria's Best Citizen in 1931 by the Native Sons of British Columbia, and became an honorary member of Women's Canadian Club of Victoria—a non-profit and non-political group interested in Canadian speakers and public affairs.

The Butchart Gardens is still open today in present-day Brentwood Bay, now boasting a coffee shop and gift shop in addition to showcasing over nine hundred varieties of plants. It has continued to evolve with the times with many achievements. In 1954 Butchart Gardens brought more tourism to Victoria than any other single attraction. For the gardens' fiftieth birthday in 1954, night lighting was installed, and in 2004, two totem poles were put up in celebration of the gardens' hundredth anniversary and to honour the traditional Coast Salish territory upon which they stand. In the same year, the gardens were also declared a National Historic Site of Canada. According to the Canadian Register of Historic Places, a database of Canadian historic sites, the gardens' "massive dimensions and dramatic aesthetic qualities represents an exceptional creative achievement in Canadian gardening history." The Victoria Symphony Orchestra has performed there, and it may be one of the most photographed gardens in North America. In summer, tourists unload off busses and scatter like seeds in the wind to explore the famous gardens. In winter, Christmas lights lie like a twinkling blanket over garden beds and hang from trees, line pathways, and shine above people gliding around on an outdoor skating rink.

For many, the joy of gardening is unmistakable. But what moves one to garden? Is it a quest for beauty? A bridge to community? A way to feel grounded and close to the earth and be self-sufficient, or a challenge to see if one can make something grow from nothing? Or is it perhaps something to do to fill the time when long days stretch out in front of us like an open road? Jennie Butchart's motivation for gardening was unusual: to cover the limestone pit eyesore next to her house.

Jennie Butchart loved gardening and she loved people. Like someone carefully combining flowers for a bouquet, Jennie combined these two passions to create and sustain The Butchart

Gardens. What started as a project to cover an unsightly excavation pit ended up as a garden with blossoms from far reaches of the earth—a charming place of great beauty that draws tourists from around the world. Jennie likely would delight in knowing that The Butchart Gardens is a top national tourist attraction that brings enjoyment to over a million visitors every year. Her memory lives on through her passion project, which blooms each spring as a tangible reminder that remarkable things can happen if action follows a vision.

CHAPTER
9

Minnie Paterson
Shipwreck Heroine

MINNIE PATERSON SCANNED the black nighttime rainforest, searching for the trail she lost among the darkness and heavy sheets of rain. She took in her surroundings by dim lantern light: shiny green salal leaves, tall sword ferns, leafless moss-covered tree branches, deep puddles of mud, and her black-and-white collie Yarrow dripping wet beside her. She needed to find the slash in a tree that marked the path, specifically a rough telegraph line trail that connected lighthouses. She was on a mission to save some shipwrecked sailors and was making her way from her lighthouse to the telegraph cabin down the coast.

She refused to let panic set in and held the lantern up in front of her, moving it around in a circle. Everything was blurry through thick curtains of rain. She was immersed in a world of mud holes and fallen trees. Her wool coat, wool hat, and long dress were heavy with water and her skin was wet and prune-like beneath

Minnie Paterson

Minnie Paterson and her dog Yarrow.
PN11869 COURTESY OF ALBERNI VALLEY
MUSEUM PHOTOGRAPH COLLECTION

her clothing. Far below her, she heard monstrous ocean waves pounding against reefs and cliffs. She took a few steps forward... and nearly tripped over a wire. Yes! The telegraph line would show her the way to the telegraph cabin. She felt her way along the wire until the lantern light revealed the expected slash on the tree. Back on the trail, she pushed onwards.

Earlier that evening, Minnie's husband, Tom, the lightkeeper at the Cape Beale lighthouse, noticed a ship at sea in obvious distress. Tom woke Minnie and they took turns watching the ship through a telescope while wind rattled the windows and walls of water crashed into the light tower. Through the telescope, Minnie and Tom saw men clinging to the ship rigging while their ship got pummelled by waves. They saw fallen masts and an upside-down flag—the international signal for distress. What they didn't know was that the lifeboats were trashed, and the men had tried, unsuccessfully, to construct a raft. What they did know was that the men were in trouble and their ship would be smashed to pieces into the ocean if someone didn't help them. The ship was the *Coloma* and it had been sailing with lumber from Port Townsend to Australia.

Normally Tom and Minnie would help ships by telegraphing to Bamfield, the small village that lay eight kilometres away. Tonight though, the telegraph line was broken from the storm; the only hope of saving the men was getting word to the *Quadra*, a government steamer that normally carried out mail, supply, and fuel deliveries as well as law enforcement. The ship, under the command of Captain Charles Hackett, was docked off Bamfield Creek at Carmanah Point—ten kilometres away from their light station at Cape Beale. Tom couldn't leave the light and foghorn, so Minnie volunteered to go. She called their collie Yarrow, grabbed a lantern, and stepped out the door. She closed the door behind her, leaving her five children and husband in the cozy, dry lightkeeper's quarters, entering a world of biting wind, sideways rain, and total darkness. If she got word to the *Quadra*, it could get to the stranded men—if she arrived before the floundering ship broke apart and the men drowned, that is.

Minnie's first obstacle was crossing the sand neck that joined their light station to Vancouver Island. It was high tide, so she had to wade for forty-five metres through frigid waist-deep water until she reached the telegraph trail. Then her hike began. She half-ran, half-walked through gale-force winds and thick rainforest. The trail was not well marked—and not much of a trail most of the time. The storm had taken down branches and turned the area into more of a pond than a forest. When the trail was visible, it was a muddy river. Minnie lost the trail and found it again several times, sometimes gripping the telegraph line to find her way, like a person clutching the railing on a wet and pitch-black staircase. The trail Minnie hiked on that night—though knee-deep mud and torrential rain—was what is now the famous West Coast Trail. Minnie desperately wanted to arrive safely at the *Quadra*. She had to. Her five children back home needed her.

Hours later and after much wet, cold, hard exertion, Minnie finally arrived at Bamfield Creek. But the rowboat that was usually there to row to the *Quadra* was not there. Her journey was not over yet. She waded through the creek, crawled through salal bushes and thick rainforest for another few kilometres. Everything in sight was coated in slippery moss—the trees, the rocks, and the ground on which she walked. The smell of mud and salt air filled her nose. She had to keep walking... or she would stop and not be able to start again. She was determined to make it to the telegraph cabin.

Shattered with exhaustion, Minnie at last dragged herself up the steps to the linesman's house. The linesman's wife, Annie McKay, a friend of Minnie's, answered the door. Shocked to see Minnie, she quickly told her that her husband was out fixing the telegraph line. Minnie relayed situation of the shipwreck to Annie, and together, they got in a small skiff and rowed through the angry sea toward the *Quadra*, taking turns to bail the rain out of the boat. Luckily, there was smoke coming out of the *Quadra*'s smokestack, a sure sign that Captain Hackett was aboard. They arrived at the ship and quickly informed him about the shipwreck off Cape Beale, and he set off immediately at full steam toward it while Minnie and Annie rowed back to shore. The fates of the stranded sailors now lay in the hands of Captain Hackett. Minnie's message was delivered, her mission complete.

Back at her cabin, Annie readied a bed and tea, assuming Minnie would stay the night and rest. Minnie accepted the tea but refused the bed, saying, "Thank you, Annie, but my baby needs me." Her youngest child was still nursing, so she left and began hiking back the way she came, with two linesmen who insisted on accompanying her. The cold set in at that point, and her core body temperature dropped drastically. Her legs cramped, likely from dehydration, exertion, and the cold. She stumbled. Her body wanted to stop moving but she forced herself to keep walking until she reached Cape Beale, where her children and husband awaited her. All in one night, she had done everything—accomplished her rescue mission and made it back home to nurse her baby.

A week later, when telegraph lines had been repaired, Minnie discovered her harrowing journey had been worth it. The *Quadra* had made it to the shipwrecked sailors just in time, moments before their ship smashed into the jagged sharp reef. All ten sailors on board had been rescued. Minnie was a heroine.

MINNIE HUFF was born in Penetanguishene, Ontario, to Eliza and Captain George Huff. George Huff played a major role in the history of the Alberni Valley, a region between modern-day Parksville and Sproat Lake, after he and Eliza moved there from Brighton, in southern Ontario. George had been a sailor on the Great Lakes and a merchant in Honduras. In 1885 he pre-empted 176 acres of land in the Alberni Valley. His business ventures were plentiful: owning and operating Alberni Valley's first store, a wharf, and a sawmill; running a boat on the Somass River, Alberni Inlet, and Kennedy Lake; building the first hall that served as a church and bank; and serving as member of parliament. Additionally, he served as mayor of the town of Alberni and brought electricity to the Valley. He also helped to build the first log-cabin school in the Alberni Valley.

Minnie spent her childhood in the Alberni Valley. If you've driven to Tofino, you've passed through Minnie's childhood hometown. Her family home was a log cabin deep in the forest. She was one of the first students in the Alberni log-cabin school. To get to school, she rowed across the Somass River in a rowboat attached to a cable. As a young woman, she met Thomas Paterson, who was from Glasgow, Scotland. They got married in 1893 and soon had a child. Thomas and Minnie lived in the Alberni Valley and owned a stable that rented out horses and buggies. Tom's work included carrying mail across Vancouver Island between Nanaimo and the Alberni Valley.

In 1895, Minnie, Thomas, and their first child moved to the lighthouse at Cape Beale, near Bamfield. Their new home was on the rugged and wild west coast of Vancouver Island. The Cape Beale lighthouse illuminated the southern entrance to Barkley Sound, located south of Ucluelet and north of Bamfield. Although Thomas was the official lightkeeper, Minnie had an active part in daily operations of the light station.

Minnie made headlines in Canada and the United States in December 1906 for her heroic hike and the rescue of men aboard the *Coloma*. A reporter from the *Seattle Times* came all the way to Bamfield to meet and interview Minnie. Captain Davies of the Sailor's Union of the Pacific gave her a framed citation, saying: "I think Mrs. Paterson is one of the last persons to think she did a heroic action, but I can tell you she is one of the best and grittiest women ever I met." From the Dominion Government, she was given a silver plate. From the officers and crew of coastal steamer *Queen City*, she was given a silver tea set, a gold locket, and a cheque for $315.15. As word of Minnie's heroic feat got around, she was nicknamed the "Grace Darling of the West Coast," after the daughter of an English lightkeeper, who similarly earned world-wide recognition after rowing out to a shipwreck and rescuing stranded men and women from the sea in 1838.

Nearly a year before Minnie's heroic hike to save the *Coloma*, she had achieved a different heroic accomplishment. The steamship *Valencia* had been sailing from San Francisco to Victoria with more than 160 passengers on board. The *Valencia* missed the entrance to the Strait of Juan de Fuca and inadvertently began heading up the west coast of Vancouver Island. Thick fog made navigation difficult, and on January 22, 1906, the *Valencia* grazed rocks about nine kilometres south of Pachena Point. The captain set the ship to full speed ahead attempting to run off the rocks. Passengers scrambled to upper decks as the ship began to break into the ocean. Some crew members were swept off to sea while attempting to operate lifeboats, and many passengers who had made it into the false security of lifeboats capsized and were lost to sea.

Tragically, most of the passengers and crew drowned. Nine men made it to shore and to a sea cave below some cliffs. They waded to shore and found a cabin beside the Darling River. They rang Cape Beale and Minnie took the call, swiftly telegraphing Victoria via Bamfield and Port Alberni with information of the shipwreck.

After this, Minnie heard her dog Yarrow bark. Minnie was eight and a half months pregnant at this time, but she ran outside and found some men in front of the light station. At first, she thought it was the same group of men who had wired her from the cabin, but she quickly realized that this was a different group of *Valencia* survivors. She invited the men inside, fed them, and kept them warm in her family's small lightkeeper's quarters. She telegraphed the linesman at Carmanah Point and instructed them to send provisions, clothing, and ropes to the men in the cabin. She and Tom stayed at the telegraph line for thirty-six hours straight, informing the government and press of the *Valencia* situation. Of the 164 passengers and crew on the *Valencia*, only thirty-seven survived. Legends tell of a ghost ship *Valencia* still haunting the coastline where it went down.

Canada and the United States both launched enquiries into the *Valencia* shipwreck, out of which eventually came a new lighthouse at Pachena Point and an extension of the Dominion Life Saving Trail, or Shipwrecked Mariners' Trail, from Port San Juan to Cape Beale. The new trail had shelters with provisions and wireless sets every ten kilometres, and regular patrols along the coastline were carried out by full-time linesmen watching out for more shipwrecks. The West Coast Trail was born.

In 1908, after thirteen years at the Cape Beale lighthouse, Minnie and Thomas moved back to the Alberni Valley. They subdivided their land and Thomas built a seven-bedroom house for them and their five children. The house still stands today, off the highway that passes through Port Alberni. Its bay windows look over the Alberni Valley's snow-capped peaks and green valleys, just as it did when the Patersons lived there. Its white paint is chipping and worn, as though it's lived through a lot. Minnie only lived in that house for five years. Her hike had given her something more sinister than awards and recognition: Her body may have been weakened from the intense nature of the hike—she developed tuberculosis and died in 1911, five years after her lifesaving trek.

Anyone who has hiked coastal trails in winter knows of their unrelentingly wet and character-building nature. Today, the West Coast Trail is a classic backpacking trip. Renowned worldwide as a stunning and historic coastal hike, thousands of people pass through it annually. Transformed from a lifesaving trail for ship-wrecked sailors to a recreational hiking route in 1973, it passes through the traditional territories of the Pacheedaht, Ditidaht, Huu-ay-aht, and Nuu-chah-nulth Peoples. Protected as a part of the Pacific Rim National Park since 1970, it remains undeveloped and wild. Although it is notoriously gruelling, it wouldn't be quite as tough as when Minnie Paterson hiked it. Today's hikers have lightweight equipment, are dressed in modern outdoor-wear, and sometimes even have the help of a professional guide. Vastly different than Minnie's solo trek—alone, at night, and in an emergency.

Minnie's story is one of courage, bravery and dedication. She is remembered as a heroine who hiked part of the famous West Coast Trail before it was a lifesaving trail or recreational hiking route. Her name and legacy live on from her epic hike, which earned her international fame, in the form of the many sailors whose lives she saved. The certificate for her award from the Sailor's Union of the Pacific states, "We, the seamen of America, fully recognize her sterling worth as the highest type of womanhood, deeply appreciating her unselfish sacrifices on behalf of those 'who go down to the sea in ships' and assure her and hers of our undying gratitude."

10

Maria Mahoi
Salt Spring Island Pioneer

MARIA MAHOI WAS a woman of the water. She loved the ocean, loved being in the water, and spent her life living on islands: Vancouver Island, Salt Spring Island, and Russell Island, a small island off Salt Spring. She lived by the sea, ate from the sea, and swam in the sea. Water was Maria's constant companion and a persistent acquaintance through every stage of her life. The ocean surrounded Maria through all the highs, lows, triumphs, and losses of her life during early days of Vancouver Island's colonial history.

Maria Mahoi was a Salt Spring Island pioneer of Coast Salish and Hawaiian descent who left an impression on her island homes for her resourcefulness and strength of spirit. The sea surrounded her throughout her life. In many ways, the sea was her life.

MUCH OF WHAT is known about Maria Mahoi is outlined in Jean Barman's book, *Maria Mahoi of the Islands*. Maria's story begins in

Young Maria Mahoi.
COURTESY OF THE SALT SPRING ISLAND
HISTORICAL SOCIETY ARCHIVES

Victoria, where many Hawaiian people arrived after leaving their tropical island homes. Hawaiian people came to Vancouver and Vancouver Island to work for the Hudson's Bay Company or for the California Gold Rush of 1848–49. Many "Kanakas," as they were called, worked as fur traders, farmers, gardeners, coopers, millwrights, or blacksmiths. "Kanaka" is the Hawaiian word for "human being." In modern contexts, the word is used to refer to a person of Native Hawaiian ancestry, and it can be found in some place names around Vancouver Island, such as Kanaka Bay on Nanaimo's Newcastle Island.

Maria Mahoi

Many Hawaiians worked for the Hudson's Bay Company on ships, in forts, and on farms. Others cleared land, built houses and hotels, or built roads. Some cleaned and processed salmon. As Barman explains in her book, Hawaiian people who had moved to the Pacific Northwest couldn't vote or own land in Oregon, so Fort Victoria and Vancouver Island, as British territories, were more appealing places to live.

Maria Mahoi was born around 1855, likely in Fort Victoria. Her father was a Native Hawaiian man named William Mahoya, who worked for the Hudson's Bay Company. Her mother was a Coast Salish woman, but very little was documented about her. It was common for Hawaiian men to marry Indigenous women. Fort Victoria was a lively HBC frontier town when Maria was born. It was bustling with land pre-emptions, the fur trade, and the gold rush. Its population was diverse and was home to various Indigenous Peoples, English, Scots, French Canadians, and Hawaiians.

In 1870 Maria began a relationship with Abel Douglas, a whaler and sea captain some years older than her. They lived together in Fort Victoria and later moved to Pasley Island, a small island west of Bowen Island. Pasley Island had a wharf and whaling camp where Abel worked. Maria learned to sail while going out aboard Abel's forty-foot schooner, the *Triumph*. Abel used the *Triumph* for trade, government services, and to fish, especially for dogfish, whose oil was used in lamps in coal mining settlements like Nanaimo. When whale oil lost its demand and petroleum took its place as a fuel, Maria and Abel left Pasley Island and moved to Salt Spring Island, where they pre-empted over a hundred acres of land near Beaver Point. They had seven children: three

sons and four daughters. On Salt Spring Island they farmed and
fished, and their children attended the Beaver Point school. Many
other Hawaiian people also lived on Salt Spring Island and nearby
Russell, Portland, and Coal Islands.

In the 1890s, though, Abel left Salt Spring Island, abandoning
Maria and their children. This put Maria in a difficult place financially as Abel was the family's main breadwinner. Maria worked
as a midwife and sent two of her daughters to stay at the St. Ann's
Residential School in Duncan. This was partly to further their
education, but also to reduce the number of mouths she had to
feed in these trying times. After Abel left Maria, she began a relationship with George Fisher, a neighbour on Salt Spring Island
and the son of a Cowichan woman and Englishman who was
some years younger than her. They got married in 1900. George
became a father figure to the children Maria had with Abel, and
together, they had six more children. George fished, did road-
work and woodwork, and worked odd jobs. Money was tight and
there was no hired help. Life was busy. Some good fortune came
to Maria in 1902 when William Haumea, a well-known Hawaiian patriarch some said was Maria's father, died and left Maria his
house and property on Russell Island, just south of Salt Spring's
Fulford Harbour. Maria couldn't read or write, so she signed the
paperwork with an X. The forty-acre island had a homestead with
established gardens and mature fruit trees. William Haumea had
been a skilled fruit grower and farmer, and the homestead fruit
crops included apples, grapes, strawberries, and peaches. Maria
and George could grow enough food to feed their family and to
sell in Victoria's Chinatown and markets on Salt Spring Island.
Maria canned much of this fruit. Cows, sheep, pigs, and chickens

rounded out their island farm. The children rowed from Russell Island to Salt Spring Island for school. Island life was calm and the family was self-sufficient.

Money was still in short supply, and it became even tighter when George, badly injured after his boat sank at sea, was bedridden and unable to work for some time. To help support the family, Maria worked as a midwife for a bit of money and would go out deer-hunting, often with a child strapped to her back. Maria mended their clothing, wove clothes from sheep's wool, and carefully preserved food from their gardens and orchards. All but one of Maria's children made it to adulthood, a rare feat in days when the rates of disease, accidents, and infant mortality were high. In 1900, George and Maria got officially married by a priest who came to Russell Island by boat from St. Ann's Church in Cowichan. According to Barman, the marriage may have been motivated by George's poor health and his unwillingness to risk dying unmarried.

Despite not being monetarily rich, Maria's life was rich with food. Traditional Coast Salish foods from the land and sea were very important to her and she taught her children to harvest and prepare them in traditional ways. They dug clams, smoked fish, and collected herring eggs. Maria smoked salmon and speared octopus with a spear George apparently made for her. She made fry bread, and the family ate asparagus, strawberries, berries, plums, and apples from their property. Maria also made fresh bread, apple pies, clam chowder, cookies, and wine from their apples and plums. George fished for dogfish, which he sometimes sold in Sidney, and on occasion, he also sold strawberries to a Salt Spring Island general store.

Years passed and Maria's children grew up. They became educated, married, and had their own children whom Maria helped bring into the world as a midwife. One of her sons fought in the First World War, hiding his Indigenous ancestry in order to serve. Her older sons from her relationship with Abel became sealers. And despite living remotely on an island, Maria was not socially isolated. She nourished many female friendships around her: Her best friend was a Hawaiian woman named Matilda Naukana, who lived on nearby Portland Island, and Maria often rowed her boat to Salt Spring Island to visit with friends, including another pioneer midwife named Mary Ann Gyves. (Read more about her in Chapter 6 of *On Their Own Terms: True Stories of Trailblazing Women of Vancouver Island*.)

Maria was a strong woman who stood her ground in the face of trouble. In her book about Maria, Jean Barman mentions a rough patch Maria and George had in their relationship. George had been with another woman, who became pregnant. Maria found out and met that woman while they worked together picking hops in Washington state. The two women apparently got into an altercation that ended with Maria throwing the other woman into a large straw basket that was used to collect hops. The other woman stayed away from George after that, was sadly thrown out by her husband, although she did get married again later. In the meantime, Maria and George mended their relationship and enjoyed tea together each afternoon at their house.

Although Maria was in a common-law relationship and later a marriage, she never took her partners' surnames, always keeping her Hawaiian surname, Mahoi. Perhaps it was her own quiet way of holding onto her Hawaiian heritage and maintaining her identity. Whatever her motivation, this was unusual for the time as the custom was for women to take their husbands' names. Either way, Maria's Hawaiian culture and language, including her belief in Hawaiian spirit guardians called tamanos, were vital to her identity. She loved paddling her canoe, sailing in her five-metre sailboat, and swimming. (Some stories about Maria even tell of her teaching her granddaughters to swim by putting them on her back.) A true woman of the islands, she even loved the wind.

MARIA MAHOI died on July 1, 1936, at her beloved home on Russell Island. She left her island property to her husband George and their children. When George died in 1948, he left the property to their daughter Mary Jane. Unfortunately, taxes became unmanageable in 1959, and she sold the Mahoi family property to a couple from California, who, in turn, sold it in 1997 to the Pacific Marine Heritage Legacy. In 2003 Russell Island became part of Gulf Islands National Park Reserve, and in 2009, Parks Canada partnered with Maria Mahoi's descendants to create a volunteer host program in which members of the Mahoi family would live in the Mahoi house for summer months, sharing their Hawaiian heritage with visitors to the island.

From the water, Russell Island looks much the same as it did when Maria lived there. Rocky shores are interspersed with white sandy beaches overhung with red-barked arbutus trees. Driftwood lies along the water's edge, discarded by the ocean and dried by scorching summer sunshine. Maria's white two-storey house still stands, its white steps welcoming visitors to a front porch with white railings. The house looks out to the orchard with apple trees that still bear sweet and juicy fruit each year, and a short kilometre-long trail circumnavigates the island.

Maria Mahoi was strong in body and spirit. She is remembered as being well-loved and hard working; always wearing a skirt, blouse, and apron; loving the water; and putting grandchildren on her back to teach them how to swim. She was tough and resilient through a challenging time in history, living through turbulent politics and rampant racial prejudice against anyone who wasn't the dominant race. She was exceptional at doing more with less. Islands were her home and the ocean her playmate, confidante, and life spirit. A prominent "Kanaka matriarch," she lived a captivating and fulsome life.

CHAPTER

11

Sylvia Stark
Pioneer

SYLVIA STARK was a courageous and independent woman who left a legacy as one of Salt Spring Island's earliest pioneers. Her family was one of the first African-American families to homestead on Salt Spring Island. The Salt Spring of Sylvia's days was vastly different than that of today. No ferries connected the island to Vancouver Island or the mainland; settlers got dropped off by steamship. When they needed supplies or staple foods that they couldn't grow themselves, they paddled across the Salish Sea to Vancouver Island, sometimes in dugout canoes and sometimes in stormy weather. Once, when Sylvia was paddling from Victoria, a storm brought fierce wind and waves that nearly capsized the dugout canoe she paddled.

Sylvia wasn't always this free. Both her parents were born into slavery in the United States and made their way to Canada's Gulf

Sylvia Stark.
COURTESY OF THE SALT SPRING ISLAND HISTORICAL SOCIETY
ARCHIVES—ESTES/STARK COLLECTION

Islands for a new life of freedom. Sylvia lived a remarkable life, chronicled by her detailed written journals.

SYLVIA ESTES was born in Clay County, Missouri, in 1839, the youngest of three children. Both her parents were enslaved—her father, Howard, to a Scotsman named Tom Estes, and her mother, Hannah, to a German baker named Charles Leopold. During this time, enslaved Black people in America usually took the surnames of their master; thus, Sylvia's parents went by the name of her father's master, Estes. This oppressive practice was standard until 1865, when slavery was abolished.

From a young age, Sylvia helped her mother with work in the Leopold bakery. Her early memories were of drying dishes and helping with the housework. Neither of her parents were literate, but Sylvia taught herself to read by learning the alphabet from one of the Leopold children and by listening in on the Leopold children's school lessons. Although her parents couldn't teach Sylvia to read, they taught her to pray. She spent much of her childhood indoors: it wasn't safe for children of colour to play outside, because of the risk of being kidnapped and sold to cotton plantations.

Howard Estes was taken with Tom Estes's sons to California, where they were to be selling a herd of cattle but also spent some time prospecting for gold. Howard was able to find enough gold to buy his and his family's freedom. He paid $1,000 each for himself, Hannah, and their son Jackson, and $900 for Sylvia. The Estes family was free to go where they pleased, and in April 1851 they moved to California by covered wagon. The six-month-long wagon trip passed with sightings of buffalo herds and swarms of locusts, snacks of sundried buffalo chips, and drinks from streams littered with cow horns and the bleached bones of animals who had died from dehydration. Sylvia picked wildflowers whenever she could. Upon arriving in their new home of California, Sylvia's father said, "We'll have to work hard, but we are working for ourselves now." Sylvia and her brother explored the hills of their new home and Sylvia picked orange California poppies. At sixteen years of age,

Sylvia met Louis Stark, a master horticulturalist who had been born in Louisville, Kentucky. He worked as a barber before buying his freedom, just as Sylvia's family had bought theirs. Sylvia and Louis got married in 1855 while in California and had two children, Willis and Emma. They would have five more children in Canada.

Despite California being a free state, injustices still existed. For example, Black Americans weren't permitted to testify in court against white people. Because of such oppressive laws, the family decided to leave the United States. James Douglas, who was at that time the governor of the colony of Vancouver Island and wanted to increase the number of pro-British settlers there, was inviting Black Americans fleeing racial discrimination and violence in the United States to settle in Canada. Sylvia and Louis, along with Sylvia's parents and siblings, also decided to go.

In 1858, thirty-five Black Americans arrived on Vancouver Island by ship. Over the next two years, six hundred more would arrive and settle. In the Colony of Vancouver Island, which included the Gulf Islands, Black people could vote, own businesses, and buy land. Of the six hundred people who arrived on the Saanich Peninsula, some moved to Victoria and others to Salt Spring Island. Sylvia's parents, Hannah and Howard, bought land in Saanich; Sylvia and Louis chose Salt Spring Island. Back then, farmers could pre-empt up to two hundred acres of land on Salt Spring Island, at a rate of $1.25 per acre. Single men could pre-empt one hundred acres, while married men two hundred acres. Women could only pre-empt land if they were widowed with dependents. The land was a wilderness, thick with trees and needing to be cleared in order to be farmed.

Sylvia Stark

In 1860 Sylvia, Louis, and their two children arrived on Salt Spring Island. As was customary back then, they were dropped by ship to their new island home. Their fifteen cows were lowered into the water with them. Sylvia was pregnant at the time. For Sylvia and Louis, who had their third child only four months after they moved, life in the wilderness on an island in the Pacific Ocean took a lot of adjustment. They were one of only six Black families living on Salt Spring Island. Their first home was an unfinished log cabin deep in the forest. They put the roof on it themselves, and before it was completed it had a quilt as a makeshift door. Additionally, no ferries serviced Salt Spring Island in those days—pioneers had to take ships or use their own boats if they wanted to leave. At first, Sylvia felt isolated and lonely. She relied on her Christian faith to keep her going as they built a homestead in the deep forest that was her new home.

Sylvia and Louis cleared their land and built a house on it. The slash and burn method of land clearing, a legal and common practice on Salt Spring Island until the 1920s, was used to turn heavily forested land into farmland. Next, oxen-powered tractors were used to plow crops, wheat and corn being most common. Sylvia ground wheat in a coffee grinder and made hominy by drying, shelling, and soaking kernels of corn. This would then be used as a thickening agent or in soups and stews. Cows, pigs, and chickens added to the family's food sources. Empty flour bags were used to mend clothing or as clothing itself. Life was not easy, and chores were constant. Their new island was also home to bears, wolves, and cougars. Smallpox epidemics came and went.

In 1870, ten years after they moved to Salt Spring Island, the Starks moved from Vesuvius Bay on the northern end of the island to Ganges, in the south. This move was prompted by mounting tensions between pioneers and the Cowichan, W̱SÁNEĆ (Saanich), Stz'uminus (Chemainus) People, who had visited or lived on the island longer than any of the new settlers. As Sylvia's second home was closer to the sea, she and the family were now able to harvest herring, mussels, and smelts. Eventually, Sylvia and her family decided to move off Salt Spring Island altogether, and in 1875, they shifted their home to Cedar in the Cranberry District of south Nanaimo, near the Chase River. Sylvia's son Willis remained on Salt Spring Island and took over the family farm. He spent his life there, rarely leaving the island and gaining a reputation as a sharpshooter cougar hunter.

In Nanaimo, Sylvia practised midwifery and prioritized her children's education. Her daughter Emma became a schoolteacher in a one-room schoolhouse in Cedar, and one of her other daughters, Marie, was one of Emma's students. Sadly, Emma died at the age of thirty-three in 1890; little has been written about the circumstances, only that she would be deeply missed as a teacher. (Read more about Emma's life in *On Their Own Terms: True Stories of Trailblazing Women of Vancouver Island.*) At the age of forty-six, Sylvia made a big move: she left her husband, left Nanaimo, and moved back to Salt Spring Island. She missed her friends, her neighbours, and the land on Salt Spring Island. Added to the list of reasons for this move was the fact that the Stark house in Nanaimo had been close to the local coal mines and daily noisy blasting. After Sylvia moved back to Salt Spring Island, though,

Sylvia Stark

Louis was suspiciously found dead at the bottom of a large cliff in Nanaimo. The year was 1895. Whispered rumours suggested a Nanaimo coal baron had killed him for his land, which was rich in coal. An inquest was launched and a detective hired, but nobody was ever charged.

SYLVIA STARK died on Salt Spring Island in 1944 and was buried in the Ganges area. She was 105 years old, likely the oldest person on Salt Spring Island at the time. A stone monument bearing the Stark name stands beside Chase River Elementary School in Nanaimo's Extension area, accompanied by an interpretive sign. Just over a fence from the interpretive sign, a barn can be seen with tired wood siding and a hunching posture that make it visibly old. The barn is part of Nanaimo's Heritage Register, and some claim it belonged to Sylvia and Louis Stark. Much of what is known about Sylvia's life was gained from detailed journals about pioneering in Nanaimo and on Salt Spring Island and from articles written by Sylvia's daughter, Maria Stark. Maria said of her mother: "She loved nature, she loved life. All nature was life to Sylvia."

CHAPTER

12

Veronica Milner
Gardener

THE TINY, BIRDHOUSE-SIZED houses in the woodland garden, all quite different from one another, belong to the fairies. Some hang suspended in the air, dangling from cedar trees. Others sit firmly among moist moss and leafy sword ferns on the sun-dappled forest floor. Stranger ones are underground dwellings, nearly buried in the soil.

This magical fairy realm is created once a year at a seaside woodland garden called Milner Gardens & Woodland. The occasion is to remember the woman who once owned the gardens: Veronica Milner, who believed in fairies.

Veronica was not the type of person you would expect to have believed in something as whimsical as fairies. She was an aristo-cratic, no-nonsense Englishwoman who loved gardening and fine china. She was far from being a free spirit, or likely believer in supernatural creatures. She was also full of surprises.

Veronica Milner

Veronica Milner's house and fairytale garden is now part
of the Milner Gardens & Woodland in Qualicum Beach.
MILNER GARDENS & WOODLAND/VIU

VERONICA VILLIERS was born in London, England, in 1909.
Winston Churchill was her mother's cousin, and Veronica was
distantly related to the ancestors of Prince Charles and Diana,
Princess of Wales. Although she came from a wealthy family, her
childhood was not a happy one. Veronica's parents were physically
and emotionally absent. Like many children of wealthy parents
back then, she was raised by nursemaids and nannies and later
attended boarding school. She was feisty and fiery, once running
away from school at night. She and a friend had planned to leave
together, but when the friend didn't show, Veronica left on her own.
She walked in the dark for several kilometres, until she reached her
grandmother's estate. Her grandmother then had her driver return
Veronica to the boarding school.

Later, Veronica attended finishing school, in France, Germany, and Switzerland. In August 1928, while at a car rally in Ireland with her brother, she met a handsome, dashing, car-obsessed Irishman named Desmond Fitzgerald, who was set to be the twenty-eighth Knight of Glin. They fell in love and were married just before Veronica turned twenty. After the wedding, they moved into Desmond's castle in Limerick, Ireland, but it wasn't the fairy-tale castle Veronica expected. It was isolated, damp, and drafty. She also butted heads with her father-in-law, who was elderly and in poor health. Desmond said Veronica was impossible and inconsiderate. At one point, she left for London, scandalously without Desmond. Divorce was not condoned back then, and the couple not only stayed married but also had three children together.

Veronica went away to England frequently, and on one trip suffered a broken leg and pelvic injury when she fell from a horse. It's fair to say she was not a happy person. Gardening and painting were her only joys in life, and even when she was in Ireland, she spent much time away from the castle, taking painting classes or painting the coastlines with other painters.

In 1944 Desmond was diagnosed with bovine tuberculosis. Veronica took him to Arizona so an American specialist could examine him, but the treatment did not work. Desmond never recovered. He was buried at his castle in Ireland after his death in 1949.

Veronica was now a single parent with three children in Ireland in a difficult economy. For money, she sold vegetables and raised chickens; in the evenings, she tended to her flower gardens. She had some suitors over the years, but didn't marry any of them. In 1954 she connected with Ray Milner, a Canadian she had met on the train when she had taken Desmond to Arizona. Ray was from Sackville, New Brunswick, and was also a widower. He had been a lieutenant in the Canadian army during the First World War, was the president of several Canadian utilities companies, and was involved in the 1954 Trans Mountain Pipeline deal. Veronica found him to be empathetic and generous. He owned property in Qualicum Beach, on Vancouver Island, which was not yet the popular retiree destination it is today. Ray chose Qualicum Beach for its moderate climate, highway access, and reputation for beautiful estates. His Qualicum Beach house (now the Milner Gardens main estate) was inspired by Sri Lankan Ceylonese tea plantation houses. It had screen doors to the outside, a bathroom for every room, and a style of eaves common to houses in monsoon climates.

Ray visited Veronica in England, where they were married a month later. Veronica was forty-five and Ray sixty-five. Veronica wore a red satin dress; her teenaged son Desmond walked her down the aisle. After the wedding, Veronica moved to Ray's estate in Qualicum Beach while her children remained in Ireland. At first, she was lonely in her new home, but the blank canvas of gardens awaited her and she wholeheartedly threw herself into designing them. Her gardening inspiration was one of William Robinson's books, *The Wild Garden*, which touted natural gardens that were wild in style. This style contrasted with the highly manicured, typical English gardens—and with Veronica's uptight, serious personality.

Ray ordered magnolia trees, lilies, azaleas, and rhododendrons from Greig Nursery in Royston. One of the nursery owners, Mary Greig, became Veronica's dear friend. Both women were from

England and shared a passion for horticulture. Veronica brought hydrangeas, beech, and eucryphia trees from her Irish castle, and Japanese maples from seeds she brought from Japan. Apparently, her Old World sycamore tree grew from a seed of the actual tree that Greek physician Hippocrates sat under. She had no formal horticultural education; she gardened solely for joy. She was a member of several societies: the American Rhododendron Society, International Dendrology Society, Vancouver Botanical Gardens Association, Royal Horticultural Society, and Royal Society of Arts and Commerce.

At that time, the existence of fairies was a popular belief in England. Some believed they were nature spirits of the forests, mountains, lakes, and rivers. Others considered them life forces that existed inherently in the natural world. Veronica's fascination with them developed from letters exchanged over the years with Shane Leslie, who had a romantic interest in her. He was a writer and was deeply interested in fairies and the supernatural. Perhaps Veronica enjoyed the idea of joyful, mischievous, and playful fairies inhabiting her garden because she didn't embody these lighthearted characteristics herself.

Ray Milner retired at eighty and passed away at eighty-six at Qualicum Beach. This was extremely difficult for Veronica. Ray was one of the only people in her life she felt truly understood her and could navigate her tempestuous personality. After his death, Veronica travelled widely, apparently with an outrageous amount of luggage. She visited Mexico, Europe, Hawaii, Ireland, and Australia.

IN 1996 VERONICA gifted Milner Gardens—which Charles and Diana, the Prince and Princess of Wales, had visited in 1986—

to Nanaimo's Vancouver Island University. Milner Gardens & Woodland seeks to preserve its heritage and contribute to the horticultural community by providing a gardening advice line and email address where gardeners can have their horticultural questions answered.

Veronica died in 1998 in her home at the age of eighty-nine. Her ashes were scattered over her garden in Qualicum Beach and her former garden in Glin, Ireland.

On summer days at Milner Gardens & Woodland, ferns and foxgloves greet you in bright sunlight; there are orchards, old-growth trees, and flowers of all sorts as far as the eye can see. Bees buzz around a hive and a Zen garden awaits walkers. An army of spry retired volunteers greets visitors at the gate and keeps Milner Gardens & Woodland going and growing. Around Christmas, it transforms into a winter wonderland with thousands of Christmas lights decorating the acres of garden pathways.

Veronica created a woodland garden with abundant unique flowers, plants, and trees. She deviated from the traditional style of English gardens in much the same way as she had deviated from the traditional English life she was born into, and created a garden whose wild natural appearance became the backdrop for a magical fairyland.

13

Barbara Touchie (Sičquuʔuƛ)
Language Champion

FOR THE FIRST years of her life, Barbara Touchie (Sičquuʔuƛ) spoke only the Barkley dialect of the Nuu-chah-nulth language. Although she would learn English and speak it throughout the rest of her life, she always remained fluent in Nuu-chah-nulth and passed her knowledge of the language on to thousands of people. She created an alphabet for the Barkley dialect of Nuu-chah-nulth and played a major role in making Nuu-chah-nulth known and accessible to the hoards of tourists who journey annually to the Tofino and Ucluelet areas of Vancouver Island.

Language is obviously central to human life, allowing people to communicate information, wants, and needs. The knowledge and wisdom embedded in language sometimes gets less credit. The knowledge of medicinal plants. Information about the land or

Barbara Touchie

Barbara Touchie.
PHOTO BY MELODY CHARLIE, COURTESY OF VI MUNDY AND FAMILY

sea. Traditional knowledge and teachings that are embraced in a language's words and phrases.

Barbara Touchie was a language champion. If you've been to Tofino or Ucluelet, maybe you've visited Parks Canada's Kwisitis Visitor Centre on Wickaninnish Beach in Pacific Rim National Park. Barbara Touchie was one of the people instrumental in the inclusion of Nuu-chah-nulth language and culture content and the richness this language and culture adds to this visitor centre today. Barbara spent years of her life revitalizing the Barkley dialect of the Nuu-chah-nulth language and making it accessible to the hundreds of thousands of tourists visiting the area she always called home.

BARBARA TOUCHIE was born in Opitsaht (across from Tofino on Meares Island) on June 20, 1931. Her mother, Ella Thompson, was a traditional drummer, singer and songwriter, and an excellent basket weaver. Her father was Joe Thompson. Barbara was the youngest and only girl of five children. Her four older brothers were forced to attend residential school, but Barbara's parents refused to let her be taken. Barbara spent her earliest years in Tofino and was later sent to live with her grandfather, Toquaht Jim, in Ucluelet. Her brothers were much older than her and had moved away to find work. Barbara spent the rest of her childhood in Hakoda Bay, now known as Stewart Bay, where her grandfather owned a small property. There were no roads connecting Ucluelet to the rest of Vancouver Island at this time. People lived off the land and sea; essentials were picked up in Port Alberni by boat.

Her grandfather, known simply as Thomson in the community, was a major influence in Barbara's childhood. He worked as a fisherman and taught his granddaughter much about Nuu-chah-nulth culture and knowledge. Along with him, the Japanese families of Ucluelet who also lived in Hakoda Bay formed a major community backdrop for Barbara's childhood. The Barkley dialect of Nuu-chah-nulth was her first language and the language she spoke throughout childhood. Although they didn't speak the same language, Barbara played for hours with the Japanese children who

106

also lived in Hakoda Bay. They devised a sort of sign language to communicate with each other and became close friends. One day a seal washed up on shore in distress, near death and in the process of giving birth. The children ran and got a nearby adult, who helped them deliver the pup. The mother seal didn't survive, but Barbara and her friends bottle fed the pup. It grew strong and the children adopted it as their pet. They named him Buster—a name all the children could pronounce no matter what language they spoke. Buster was tame and friendly and played with the children in the water. He would even come when they called him. Barbara remembered those times fondly throughout her life.

Along with happy memories, there were some painful ones too. During the Second World War, Japanese Canadians were taken to internment camps, often never to return to their homes before being interned. Barbara remembered the day government officials came to take away the Japanese-Canadian families of Ucluelet, seizing their boats and houses as well. Young Barbara watched as Japanese women cried and frantically hid dishes, cups, and silverware in the walls of their houses. The men buried their tools and fishing gear in the ground, hoping to retrieve them later. They could take with them only what they could carry. Barbara remembered being confused and scared, worriedly asking her grandfather questions: What was happening? Was she going to be taken away too?

Many Japanese Canadians didn't return to Canada's west coast. Those who did often found that their houses and boats had been sold. Years after the Second World War was over, delicate china cups and plates were discovered in the walls of houses in Ucluelet's former Japanese settlement; tools and fishing gear were unearthed during archaeological digs—material reminders of the deeply unjust treatment of Japanese Canadians, many of whom were born in Canada.

After Barbara's coming of age, she married a man her mother chose for her. Barbara was one of the last women in her community to have an arranged marriage, which in her culture involved a woman's mother choosing a husband she found suitable for her daughter. Samuel Touchie was the man Barbara's mother chose for her, and she was confident that he would be a virtuous husband. And as it turned out, she was right! Barbara and Sam's eldest daughter, Vi Mundy, remembers her parents having a solid partnership. They had fifteen children, eight daughters and seven sons, that they raised together. They both had the same ideas about parenting and never once argued in front of the children. Family teachings included respecting oneself and one's elders, listening with the heart, helping one another, especially elders, getting up early, being involved in the community, helping with activities and cleanup at community gatherings, helping in the house, learning to cook, and other basic life skills. The children were taught to be independent and not rely on others to take care of them. Sam also supported Barbara working outside of the home—not a common decision for a woman at that time.

Barbara's work included sitting on council for the Ucluelet First Nation. She was involved in housing and did a lot of work with setting up the membership code—a list of all Ucluelet First Nation members. Her work also largely involved language, much of which was done when she was between sixty-five and eighty-three years old. She dedicated forty years of her life to revitalizing and sharing the Nuu-chah-nulth language and culture in and around Tofino. In the 1990s she and several other women developed an alphabet for the Barkley dialect of the Nuu-chah-nulth language. It was important that fluent speakers did this job. Together, the group created the forty-four symbols that represent the written form of the language.

For the next twenty-five years Barbara worked with Parks Canada to make Nuu-chah-nulth language and culture visible to the hundreds of thousands of tourists who visit Tofino and Ucluelet annually. Between 2007 and 2011, she was also one of the instrumental members of the Nuu-chah-nulth Working Group, which advised Parks Canada with traditional knowledge and cultural guidance during renovations of the Kwisitis Visitor Centre (formerly the Wickaninnish Interpretive Centre) in Ucluelet. She played a major role in updates to the centre, making sure the Nuu-chah-nulth People's history, language, culture was represented there. Her life and work is honoured in an exhibit that still stands in the centre today.

One of the last major projects Barbara worked on was translating the David Suzuki Foundation's values—the Declaration of Interdependence—into Nuu-chah-nulth. This declaration discusses the interconnectedness of life and pledges to change the relationship between humanity and the Earth, with the hopes of inspiring people to live more lightly and mindfully on the earth.

Barbara became a widow at the age of forty-four, when her husband, Sam, died of a heart attack. She was often asked by her daughters if she would remarry and always said she had no desire to. She said she was quite happy as she was. There were other challenges she faced through her life, including major changes in society over the years and the passing of her children in her later years. Her daughter Vi said she never saw her mother fall apart and that her strong values and teachings from her grandfather kept her going through hardships. Her grandfather's teachings included keeping healthy and active, avoiding being idle, participating actively in your community, and the notion that death is a part of life. Barbara's grandfather, well regarded in the community, was one of her strongest role models and a source of strength and inspiration. A healthy life was of tremendous importance to Barbara, and she practised this with beach walks for exercise, spending time with family, eating traditional food—including fish, clams, crab, and mussels—and keeping busy and active in her community.

When asked what Barbara would have thought of the issues facing society today, her daughter Vi said Barbara would have been interested in how our world has changed, how younger people are attaining more education nowadays and how women and girls are progressing and becoming vocal in different issues. Vi thinks her mother would have recommended that people make it their business to find out what's going on in our world, and if they don't like it, they should either adapt somehow or to go out and make changes. She would have told young people to find out their identity, to maintain their identity, to learn and keep up the teachings of their family, and to live a healthy life. She would have told young people today to be aware. Aware of what's going on around them. Aware of things that are changing. To roll with whatever is happening around them. And if they don't like what's going on, make it their business to learn even more.

Barbara Touchie

BARBARA PASSED AWAY in 2014 at the age of eighty-three. She had been healthy until only months before she passed; the only times she spent in hospital were when having her babies. Her daughter Vi Mundy remembers her as being strong emotionally and always community minded. Barbara's proudest life accomplishments were her children. She was proud that they never forgot their teachings, that they were early risers like their father, and that they always worked to be self-sufficient and live within their means; she was proud that they always helped where they could, assisting Elders with wood or other physical chores; and she was proud that they looked out for their community and for families who needed support. Vi Mundy is herself a leader in her community, having served two consecutive terms as chief counsellor of the Ucluelet First Nation and helped with historical research and treaty negotiations. She helped negotiate the historic Maa-nulth First Nations' Final Agreement in 2007.

Barbara's happiest times were during her childhood in Hakoda Bay, playing with her Japanese-Canadian friends, and also when her children started having babies of their own and she entered the world of grandparenthood. She was overjoyed to be a grandmother.

Barbara Touchie is remembered as being incredibly progressive and forward-thinking, and was considered to be "way ahead of her time." She is also remembered as a patient and kind teacher while teaching words and sounds of the Nuu-chah-nulth language to new learners.

As a key person in the preservation and revitalization of Nuu-chah-nulth culture and language, Barbara Touchie left a strong legacy. With her cultural and linguistic knowledge and strength of spirit, she was able to preserve, teach, and share the

Nuu-chah-nulth language, which in turn, has made it possible for others to further preserve the traditions, knowledge, and wisdom of the Nuu-chah-nulth People within the language and passed on to thousands of people. Barbara's name lives on. She is honoured at language ceremonies, including the "Let the Languages Live" conference in Victoria, BC, that celebrated 2019 as the International Year of Indigenous Languages. A Parks Canada exhibit is dedicated to her, and in 2005 Parks held a celebration honouring her by naming a theatre after her. Barbara's voice literally lives on as one of the voices heard on the First Voices Indigenous language app for the Barkley dialect of the Nuu-chah-nulth language. Even now, Barbara is teaching the Nuu-chah-nulth language.

14

Edith Berkeley
Marine Biologist and
Academic Researcher

IN 1919 Edith Berkeley arrived in the coal mining town of Nanaimo, BC, to study marine worms. Despite having attending London University, where she earned a degree in zoology, she was not permitted to be staff and had to settle instead for being a volunteer investigator at the Pacific Biological Station in Nanaimo's Departure Bay. At this time, it was not common for women to take up government research jobs or positions in academia.

Edith was undaunted by her demotion to volunteer researcher. In many ways, being a volunteer afforded her more freedom than being a female staff member. She was able to conduct research, do field work, and publish her work freely, despite being married, whereas paid female staff were expected to stop working if they married. She made the absolute most of the opportunities she

Edith Berkeley.
COURTESY OF THE UNIVERSITY OF SASKATCHEWAN
ARCHIVES SPECIAL COLLECTIONS

had; in fact, she became a world authority on marine polychaetes (marine worms).

Edith's research on marine worms in the waters off Nanaimo led to her publishing twelve papers as sole author and thirty-four with her husband, Cyril, as co-author. She revelled in studying worms previously never studied—some from depths of up to nearly five kilometres. Her research put the Pacific Biological Station on the map and contributed to the growth in its reputation. Many female researchers of this time had to publish their work under their husbands' names, but Edith published much of her work under her own name. Cyril joined her research in 1930, but Edith was the driving force.

EDITH DUNINGTON was born in 1875, in Tulbagh, South Africa, to English parents. As a teenager, she travelled solo from Tasmania to England through Cape Horn. She was headed to London University to pursue a scholarship in pre-medical studies, although partway through her studies she switched to chemistry and zoology. While at university, Edith met Cyril Berkeley, a fellow student from London, England, in the most classic, pre-Tinder, almost-out-of-a-movie sort of way—by bumping into each other at a hallway corner, each carrying an armful of books.

Cyril and Edith married in 1902 and moved to the Bihar region of India after they both graduated. Cyril's chemistry work involved processing the green leaves of the indigo plant into blue dye for clothing such as blue jeans. In 1903 their daughter, Alfreda, who would be their only child, was born in a village called Sirsi. Alfreda lived with her parents for a year and then (as was customary in that day for children whose parents were working abroad) went to live with her grandmother in England. Edith and Cyril continued to live and work in India for twelve years until the climate, with its cyclical monsoons, became too much for them to bear.

In 1914 the couple moved to Lavington, just outside Vernon in BC's Okanagan Valley. There they farmed a ranch and taught at the newly founded University of British Columbia. Edith taught zoology and Cyril bacteriology. Eventually they came to a realization: They were good ranchers, but their hearts were in research. In 1919 they moved again, this time to Nanaimo, BC, where they both started doing research—Edith doing so on a volunteer basis—out of the Pacific Biological Station. This federal marine research station opened in 1908 on the shores of Departure Bay. Departure Bay is best known these days for its bustling ferry terminal, but the Pacific Biological Station still operates as a federal marine research station in its original location. Edith had left a paid, dependable position as a professor to be an unpaid researcher. She followed her passion, even if it wasn't the easiest or most secure path to take.

Edith's research on marine polychaetes was relevant for several reasons. These marine worms have existed in the Earth's oceans for millions of years and are a vital food source for fish and birds. They also play an unexpected role in climate change and protecting the ozone layer. When marine worms turn organic debris from the ocean floor into carbon dioxide they make it available to phytoplankton, which helps reduce the amount of atmospheric carbon dioxide. If only she had known what a big issue that would be in the twenty-first century.

Following in her mother's footsteps, Alfreda Needler became a marine biologist, earning a doctorate from the University of Toronto and studying west coast shrimp, east coast oysters, and red tide. Alfreda's daughter Mary Needler Arai was a third-generation marine biologist, becoming a professor at the University of Calgary and receiving a Lifetime Achievement Award in Hiroshima, Japan, for her jellyfish research. In 1951 Alfreda passed away prematurely. This devastated Edith, but she continued focusing on her research.

Edith Berkeley

She and Cyril lived in their beloved Departure Bay, or "the bay" as they called it, until their deaths.

EDITH DIED IN 1963 in Nanaimo, at the age of eighty-seven. Cyril also passed away in Nanaimo, but not until 1973. Edith conducted research until the end of her life. Her talent and passion for marine biology were admirable and inspiring, paving the way for future female marine biologists. Several species were named in her honour, including the Berkeley eualid or Berkeley's shrimp (*Eualus berkeleyorum*), a small red shrimp with a bent tail and distinct bands around its abdomen.

15

Mary
Ellen Smith

Politician

POLITICS IS LIKELY not the first thing that comes to mind when you think of Nanaimo, British Columbia. Perhaps you envision bustling ferry terminals, horse-drawn coal carts, or royal blue water in a calm harbour, a slow boat gliding through and a seal's black dog-like head peeking above the surface. Or maybe you imagine biting into a chocolatey, custard-filled Nanaimo bar. Not politics, though. Although Nanaimo might not be readily associated with politics, the city was home to a trailblazing politician and suffragist named Mary Ellen Smith.

Mary Ellen Smith was the first of many things: she was the first woman to become a Member of the Legislative Assembly (MLA) in British Columbia and the first woman in the British Empire to become a cabinet minister and a Speaker.

Mary Ellen Smith

Mary Ellen Smith.
COURTESY OF CITY OF VANCOUVER ARCHIVES,
CVA 289-046, GEORGE T. WADDS

MARY ELLEN SMITH was born Mary Ellen Spear in Tavistock, southern England in 1863. Her mother was Mary Ann Spear and her father was a copper miner named Richard Jackson Spear. She attended school in Northumberland, attained teacher training, and became an elementary school teacher. She loved music, singing, and drama.

In 1883, Mary Ellen married a man named Ralph Smith, and in 1892 the couple moved to Canada, settling in Nanaimo, British Columbia, where Ralph worked first as a coal miner and then as a preacher. Over the years, Mary Ellen and Ralph had five children—a daughter and four sons—and Ralph eventually became very involved with the early mine unions. Union work led him to politics, and by 1916 he was the Minister of Finance for the Legislative Assembly of British Columbia. Mary Ellen helped him campaign and would sometimes give his speeches if he wasn't able to make a speaking engagement. Some said she even wrote his speeches.

In 1917 two unprecedented things happened: women got the right to vote, and Mary Ellen's husband died suddenly of appendicitis. Mary Ellen decided to run in the by-election as an Independent Liberal. She won by a large margin. In fact, she won by the largest majority by a candidate to date. With this, she took her husband's spot in the legislature under Premier John Oliver. This was historic for British Columbia and Canada. Mary Ellen was the first woman in the British Empire to be in the legislature. On her first day at work on February 7, 1918, she received the greatest ovation ever shown to a new member of the BC Legislature. In her first speech, on March 11, she stated, "I have come to you neither with a chip on my shoulder nor with a sword in my hand, but with a willingness to meet you on equal ground as representatives of the people."

In 1920 Mary Ellen, running for the Liberal Party, was re-elected as an MLA by a large margin once again, and in 1921 she was appointed to John Oliver's cabinet as minister without portfolio. Once more, she made history as the first woman in the British Empire to hold the rank. Ministers without portfolio are government officials who are given a ministerial rank without having specific areas of responsibility and who can assist with any parliamentary department.

Mary Ellen was offered the Speaker's chair in 1921 but she declined, choosing to remain as an MLA so she could accomplish more positive social change. She stuck to her beliefs and thought that everyone, including politicians, should be true to themselves, stating that she "would rather go to jail for a principle than go through life in a gilded cage without principle." Freedom and authenticity were far more significant to Mary Ellen than luxury and superficiality.

An interesting opportunity presented itself in 1923 when Mary Ellen travelled to England as a representative for the Dominion's Immigration Department. Her job was to convince the people of England to move to Canada for work. This was to increase immigration to Canada.

In 1924 Mary Ellen ran for office again. She won again, but only by a small margin this time. When she ran again in 1928, she lost to the Conservative representative. She was in her sixties by this time and wasn't asked by her party to run again. She remained politically involved, though, and in 1929 was a Canadian delegate for the International Labor Organization. Though retired from public office, she also stayed on as the president of the BC Liberal Party. She kept this role until her death.

Another opportunity to be the Speaker of the BC Legislature arrived when Mary Ellen was asked to take the place of John Andrew Buckham, who was going on leave. Another historic milestone, she took the post on February 22, 1928, the first female Speaker in Canada and the British Empire. At first, other MLAs fumbled over their words, having to adjust from saying "Mr. Speaker" to "Madam Speaker." They soon adapted.

Mary Ellen established herself in her new role and became known as a quick thinker. As Speaker, Mary Ellen soon "mastered the intricacies of political compromise and was equipped not only to carry on her husband's work, but to make a considerable name for herself. She was on equal footing with men and could take the chair at a convention and give any man in the party points both in procedure and transaction of business."

Social reform was Mary Ellen's political vision. Jan Peterson describes Mary Ellen's political work in her book *Harbour City: Nanaimo in Transition, 1920–1967*. Mary Ellen worked hard to help pass the Minimum Wage Act in 1918, which fixed a minimum wage for women at $12.77 a week. Mary Ellen also helped pass the Mothers' Pension Act in 1924, later to be called Mothers' Allowances Act in 1937. This ensured divorced or deserted wives or widows had assured income with which to raise children under sixteen years old. A widow with one child could get up to $42.50 per month with each additional child bringing in an additional $7.50. Similarly, Mary Ellen helped establish the Deserted Wives Maintenance Act, which ensured single mothers had sufficient income to support their children. Mary Ellen firmly believed that government should be predominantly about the social needs of people, including women and children. She also fought for funding for nurses, maternity benefits, and old age pension, and helped establish juvenile courts in British Columbia. And she endorsed proportional representation, a democratic principle that seeks for the seats a political party gains to reflect the number of people who voted for that party. Although she was a member of the Liberal Party of BC, Mary Ellen firmly believed that non-partisan politics was the best route to support women and children.

Mary Ellen wasn't a hit everywhere she went, though. She wasn't always progressive in her politics and supported eugenics and troubling legislation against Asian people and people with mental health disorders. Many of her views were outright racist.

Mary Ellen Smith

MARY ELLEN died of a stroke in 1933 at the age of seventy-two. She was living in Vancouver, having moved there with her husband in 1911. Her involvement in her community reached far past her political work. She was a women's suffragist well before becoming involved in politics, and she was deeply involved in a variety of groups and causes throughout her life. She was the vice-president of the Nanaimo Hospital Women's Auxiliary, the president of the Women's Canada Club and the Women's Forum, a member of the Dominion Board of Mental Hygiene, regent for the Vancouver chapter of the Imperial Order of the Daughters of the Empire, and established the Laurier Liberal Ladies' League. Mary Ellen Smith was all about improving living and working conditions for women and girls in British Columbia.

Mary Ellen's name still carries weight years after her death. As proposals were made for the BC Government to make drastic changes to the foster home program and move to the village program, it was suggested to name some of the villages after Mary Ellen, the first female MLA in Canada and a woman who fought tirelessly for social reforms that would benefit women and children. The University of Waterloo also honoured Mary Ellen in a suffrage research collection of archival material. And in north Nanaimo, Mary Ellen Drive, which connects Dover Bay Road with the Island Highway, pays homage to her. Look for this street just as you're passing Woodgrove Mall in north Nanaimo.

First-wave feminists in Canada fought for women to have the right to vote, for labour and health rights, and for legal recognition as persons. Mary Ellen did all these things and more. And in many ways, she was on her own. She didn't have any women's liberation movements behind her (because she helped establish some of them), nor did she have the online community or instant access on social media to other progressive women leaders. She lived well before days of the Internet and social media. In a time when "it was looked upon as vulgar for a lady to have any political views," Mary Ellen fought to be heard. A champion of women's rights, she once stated: "People are realizing as never before that women's tongues count for something, after all, in public life."

So next time you catch a ferry to or from Nanaimo, or wander along its peaceful, picturesque waterfront, think about one more thing: that it was home to a political trailblazer—a woman who was deeply committed to improving the lives of women and children, and who went far beyond her civic duty of voting to become the first female MLA, cabinet minister, and Speaker not just in British Columbia, but in Canada and the British Empire.

CHAPTER

16

Pansy May Stuttard
Coastal Skipper, Nurse, and Madam

AT VANCOUVER ISLAND'S northern tip, an island shelters a sandy cove from rough seas. That sandy cove is Sea Otter Cove and the island is Helen Island. Despite its proximity to San Josef Bay and Cape Scott Provincial Park—popular camping and hiking destinations—few people venture to Sea Otter Cove these days. It is lonely and deserted, with only the very occasional hiker, sea kayaker, and boater venturing to its shores. But Sea Otter Cove was once a happening place. Land pre-emptions in the San Josef Bay area meant there were settlers, and significantly more ship traffic and fishermen than today. And this meant demand for booze and brothels. A woman named Pansy May saw an opportunity there for a business venture and grabbed it.

PANSY MAY MILLER was born in Syracuse, New York, on December 27, 1875. She had three siblings. When Pansy was nineteen years old,

Pansy May Stuttard.
COURTESY OF DELTA HERITAGE SOCIETY AND CITY OF DELTA

she gave birth to a baby girl she named Nahmeoki Shaw DeJune. The baby's father was Louis Bartley DeJune, who Pansy married in New York City in 1893, a year after Nahmeoki's birth. For reasons unknown, Pansy and Louis divorced in 1900. Divorce was neither common nor well accepted in the 1900s, but Pansy wasn't the type to care. By this time, she was twenty-five. Louis remained in New York, later marrying another woman in Toronto. Nahmeoki passed away in Vancouver at twenty-eight from influenza.

After the divorce, Pansy joined the Red Cross, beginning a seven-year career as a nurse (she had graduated from the nursing program at St. Luke's Hospital in New York City in 1898), during which she travelled and saw the world through flu and smallpox epidemics, the Spanish–American War, and the building of the Panama Canal.

In 1905, Pansy moved to Vancouver, British Columbia, and in May 1909 she married Rupert Stuttard, a thirty-six-year-old sea captain from England. Both lived in Vancouver's South Hill area and that's where they were married. Together, they bought five boats and started a coastal freight business, delivering supplies to mines and remote camps on the BC coast that were unserved by other boats. Their fleet headquarters was at Sea Otter Cove, near Cape Scott on the north coast of Vancouver Island. Pansy worked on the boats, including some outside of her freight business (a passenger ship that travelled between Vancouver and Sechelt, for example). Eventually, she became the first woman in Canada to earn a coastal water skipper's ticket, a very unusual qualification for a woman at the time. Pansy made good use of her ticket, working up and down the Pacific Northwest coast, from Vancouver to Alaska. In remote places that lacked medical services, she would leave the boat to perform nursing duties if someone was in need of medical attention. In *Cape Scott and the North Coast Trail: Hiking Vancouver Island's Wildest Coast*, Maria Bremner says Pansy was well liked by settlers and even delivered a baby for a well-known Cape Scott settler family, the Rasmussens.

Back then, boating, bootlegging, and brothels went hand in hand. Pansy recognized that she could profit from all three simultaneously. In 1911 she opened a brothel on Helen Island, near Sea Otter Cove, which fishermen and loggers frequented. Brothels at that time were referred to as "blind pig's inns," saloons that stayed open late and served alcohol without permits, although the authorities "turned a blind eye to [these] happenings." They also went by many other names in the early 1900s: houses of ill repute, boarding houses, rooming houses, speakeasies, and Turkish baths. Moral reformers of the day called them moral ulcers. After Sea Otter Cove, Pansy owned five brothels that she called cabarets in Vancouver. She became known as Pansy May Cabaret, but was also called Hulda May or Momma May. Her brothels may have been on Shore Street, but it's difficult to know for sure, as red-light districts frequently moved locations within cities. Brothel owners had to be tough. They endured violent customers, fights, frequent fines, and recurring police raids. After police raids, Pansy's cabaret would be temporarily shut down while she appeared in court, paid fines, and went back to running the brothel. This was common practice, as the fines that brothels brought in were large income generators for cities and even viewed by some as unofficial business licences.

In the 1920s, Pansy eventually moved out of Vancouver to the Tsawwassen peninsula. She bought twenty-seven acres of land, ten of which were beside the American border and along Tsawwassen Beach. It was here that she launched one of her other business ventures: an Angora goat farm. Her initial plan was to raise the three goats she purchased in Texas and breed them to be shown in exhibitions. Instead, the three goats multiplied into a herd of sixty-two Angora goats that Pansy used for wool. If nothing else, Pansy May could adapt. But even her goat farm business landed her in court. She was taken to court for apparently pointing a rifle at a policeman when he came to her goat farm. Speaking in court, she claimed she was carrying a gun to protect her Angora goat kids from eagles and went on to say that if she had pointed the gun at the policemen, "he wouldn't be here and I wouldn't either." The case was thrown out of court.

Pansy lived in an enormous slab-and-log finished house on her property and, across from this, she built a larger building that would be her cabaret, dance hall, and brothel, with sixteen rooms available for rent and lots of space to host wild parties. The property was strategically situated next to the border to the United States, where prohibition was still in effect. Bootlegging alcohol from Canada was very illegal but also very profitable.

The isolated, forested nature of her Tsawwassen property made it an ideal brothel and bootlegging location. American fishermen and cannery workers from Point Roberts, on the very southern tip of the Tsawwassen Peninsula, would purchase alcohol from the cabaret or Pansy's back door. A cable and pulley system from her house to water below allowed her to sell cases of liquor on an even larger scale to boats that delivered the liquor other places. Later, she devised a staircase down to the beach to get liquor cases to waiting boats.

Local residents were unhappy with Pansy's cabaret. Unimpressed with goings on at the property, they launched numerous petitions against her, hoping to shut down her establishment. Pansy's thoughts were that in her area there were "too many churches, too few people." Ultimately, the end of prohibition in America in 1933 signalled the end of her lucrative cabaret and bootlegging businesses.

When her land in Tsawwassen was bought up to install underground hydro lines to Vancouver Island, Pansy moved to White Rock, where she spent her retirement with her cocker spaniel and the stuffed trophy animals she had shot. There were bear rugs, deer, caribou, moose, and a cougar she shot in the Capilano Canyon. She told people the oil paintings in her house were hers from when she attended art school. She had dropped out because she preferred landscape painting to the regimented techniques and "straight lines" they taught in school.

When Pansy was eighty-four years old, she made front page news. In an article in the *Lethbridge Herald* on January 4, 1958, titled "No Mood to Die," she told reporters two robbers had crashed into her bedroom at 3:00 AM, tying her hands with electrical cord and shaking her upside down so the $15,000 she had pinned in a towel under her nightgown fell onto the floor. The money must have come from selling her Tsawwassen property and she apparently didn't trust banks to keep it safe. The thieves seized the money and left. After untying herself, Pansy fired two shots from her 12-gauge shotgun at them and chased them down the street. In the aftermath of a previous robbery that also made the front pages, she had told reporters about suffering a blow to her head and being found in her house four days later. The person who found her apparently called a hearse, an ambulance, and a priest. Pansy proudly said, "I've got the bill for the hearse in my drawer... but I'm going to live to be 100. The Lord won't take me, and the devil don't want me." In her later years, Pansy lived alone and gardened. She often told people she had no regrets about her life.

PANSY MAY STUTTARD died in Surrey in 1963 at the age of eighty-nine. She was a force to be reckoned with, having been a nurse, an entrepreneur, a goat farmer, and the first woman in Canada to earn a coastal water skipper's ticket. Some of her chosen careers were high-risk and illegal; others were utterly outlandish. Imagine the yet untold tales of Pansy's unapologetic, though perhaps unethical, and unorthodox life!

Conclusion

THROUGH THESE STORIES you've met more trailblazing women from Vancouver Island's southern tip in Victoria to its very north at Sea Otter Cove. I hope you've enjoyed these stories of women who flourished on Vancouver Island. Stories define us and captivate us. The women in these stories didn't follow the dominant tropes of their time. Some of them were wild, others quietly brave. Courageously, they defined their own life stories. And when their narratives got challenging, they adapted and got on with their lives. They kept going.

A common thread woven through all these stories is the way the women made themselves the narrators of their stories. They refused to let others choose what words made up their lives. Despite many of them being born into cultures that valued and empowered men over women, they did as they pleased. They took control of their own life accounts.

A person's story rarely unfolds in isolation. The overlapping of two women's profiles was a fascinating part of researching and writing this book. When I found out two women had known each other, I imagined life stories overlapping like two intersecting paths on a forest trail. Sometimes the paths might go side by side for quite some time. Other stories crossed briefly and then proceeded their separate ways. Amelia Connolly Douglas, Isabella Mainville Ross, and Josette Legacé Work were companions in Fort Victoria's early days. Maria Mahoi paddled from Russell Island to Salt Spring Island to visit her dear friend Mary Gyves, who was featured in *On Their Own Terms*. Other links between this book and *On Their Own Terms* include the close friendship of Emily Carr and Edythe Hembroff-Schleicher, as well as the portraits that Hannah Maynard took of Amelia Connolly Douglas. And then there were connections that were hinted at but not confirmed: Did Mary Ellen Smith and Edith Berkeley's paths cross? Both women resided in Nanaimo around the same time and some research I discovered suggested that Mary Ellen attended the Pacific Biological Station's opening in 1908. Perhaps they were even friends, oblivious that decades after their days in Nanaimo they would both have city streets bearing their names? These connections confirm that our stories don't occur in a vacuum and, like waves causing ripples through a calm lake, often influence and involve other people.

I hope these women's stories have inspired you to examine your own story, to be proud of it, or to give voice to it—or perhaps to change the narrative if it doesn't serve you anymore. Vancouver Island's history was made richer by these women's stories. Their stories aren't women's history; they're simply history. I hope that these accounts have added some flourish to your life and inspired you to flourish in your own way.

Bibliography and References

Mary Ann Croft

Ahrens, R.H. Memorandum, August 4, 1972. "Discovery Island Marine Park."
Historical Documents. Discovery Island Website. Accessed March 25, 2020. https://
www.discoveryisland.ca/apps/photos/photo?photoid=198272429.

British Colonist. "Discovery Island Gift Now Officially a Park," July 29, 1972.

———. "Discovery Island Lightkeeper Succors Old Man Almost Dead From Privation,"
October 22, 1909.

Croft, Mary Ann. Letter to Ralph Smith, March 11, 1911. *Historical Documents.*
Discovery Island Website. Accessed March 25, 2020. https://www.discoveryisland.
ca/apps/photos/photo?photoid=60847192.

Discovery Island. 2004. "Discovery Island," Accessed March 25, 2020. https://www.
discoveryisland.ca.

Johnson, Peter, John Walls, and Richard Paddle (photog.). *To the Lighthouse: An
Explorer's Guide to the Island Lighthouses of Southwestern BC.* Victoria: Heritage
House Publishing, 2015.

Leah Rae. "Women Lightkeepers, Heroes by the Sea: A Co-lab Challenge," March
12, 2020. Library and Archives Blog. Accessed March 25, 2020. https://
thediscoverblog.com/tag/mary-croft/.

Lighthouse Friends. "Discovery Island, B.C," 2020. Accessed March 25, 2020. https://
www.lighthousefriends.com/light.asp?ID=1180.

Victoria Chung

Conn, David. *Raincoast Chronicles 22: Saving Salmon, Sailors and Souls.* Madeira Park,
BC: Harbour Publishing, 2013.

Forster, Merna. *100 More Canadian Heroines: Famous and Forgotten Faces*. Toronto: Dundurn, 2001.

Humphreys, Danda. *On the Street Where You Live: Sailors, Solicitors and Stargazers of Early Victoria*. Victoria: Heritage House Publishing, 2001.

Peterborough Examiner. "Chinese Woman Doctor to Give Address in City," February 14, 1948.

Price, John and Ningping Yu. *A Woman in Between: Searching for Dr. Victoria Chung*. Vancouver: Chinese Canadian Historical Society of British Columbia, 2019.

Wong, May Q. *City in Colour: Rediscovered Stories of Victoria's Multicultural Past*. Victoria: TouchWood Editions, 2018.

Yee, Paul. *Chinatown: An Illustrated History of the Chinese Communities of Victoria, Vancouver, Calgary, Edmonton, Winnipeg, Toronto, Montreal and Halifax*. Toronto: James Lorimer & Company, 2005.

Amelia Connolly Douglas

Adams, John. *Old Square-Toes and His Lady: The Life of James and Amelia Douglas*. Victoria: Touchwood Editions, 2011.

Gould, Jan. *Women of British Columbia*. Saanichton, BC: Hancock House Publishers, 1975.

Heroines.ca. "Amelia Douglas (1812–1890): Fur Trade Pioneer." Accessed January 25, 2020. http://www.heroines.ca/people/douglas.html

Milburn, Elizabeth. "First Lady," *Westward Magazine*. March-April 1980.

Wong, May Q. *City in Colour: Rediscovered Stories of Victoria's Multicultural Past*. Victoria: TouchWood Editions, 2018.

Edythe Hembroff-Schleicher

BC BookWorld. "Hembroff-Schleicher, Edythe." Accessed March 21, 2020. https://abcbookworld.com/writer/hembroff-schleicher-edythe/.

Duffus, Maureen. "Author-Artist Exhibits Work at Gallery." *Victoria Daily Times*, September 4, 1969.

Feckless: A Historical Collection of British Columbia Art. "Edythe Hembroff-Schleicer, 1906–1994." Accessed March 24, 2020. https://www.fecklesscollection.ca/edythe-hembroffschleicher.

Forbes, Vivian. Letter to Edythe Hembroff-Schleicher, Dec 8, 1972.

Hembroff-Schleicher, Edythe. *Emily Carr: The Untold Story*. Surrey: Hancock House, 1978.

———. *M.E: A Portrayal of Emily Carr*. Toronto: Clarke, Irwin Company, 1969.

———. Letter to Canada Council for the Arts, October 28, 1973.

———. Letter to Doris Schadbolt, October 4, 1971.

———. Letter to Nancy Ryley, September 18, 1973.

———. Letter to Ruth DonCarlos, January 29, 1974.

———. Letter to Tony Emery, December 14, 1973.

Lort, Kit. "Repatriating Emily." *Monday Magazine*. December 15–21, 1978.

O'Hanlon, Barbara. "The Emily Carr Story by her Friend." *The Vancouver Courier*. November 30, 1978.

Ryley, Nancy. Letter to Edythe Hembroff-Schleicher, November 2, 1973.

Smart, Amy. "Edythe Hembroff-Schleicher: Portrait of Emily Carr's Friend." *Times Colonist*. June 28, 2013.

Stockstill, Heather. "Ex-companion retraces Carr Travels." *The Whitehorse Star*. June 20, 1980.

Isabella Mainville Ross

Clark, Cecil. "Yesterday, Today." *The Victorian*, no. 697 (February 23, 1977).

Gould, Jan. *Women of British Columbia*. Surrey: Hancock House Publishers, 1975.

Goulet, George and Terry Goulet. "Isabella Mainville Ross: First Female Métis Pioneer of Victoria," June 2014. British Columbia Métis Federation website. Accessed March 18, 2020. http://bcmetis.com/wp-content/uploads/Ross.Profile.pdf.

Hilts, Marvin and Richard Brammer. "Isabella Mainville Ross." Find a Grave website, August 24, 2008. Accessed March 18, 2020. https://www.findagrave.com/memorial/29269739/isabella-ross#source.

Powell, Jay and Sam Sullivan. "Chinook Wawa." *Canadian Encyclopedia*, February 6, 2006. Accessed March 20, 2010. https://www.thecanadian encyclopedia.ca/en/article/chinook-jargon.

Watts, Richard. "The Woman Behind Ross Bay." *Times Colonist*. June 20, 2013. Accessed on March 20, 2020. https://www.timescolonist.com/the-woman-behind-ross-bay-1.327547.

Wong, May Q. *City in Colour: Rediscovered Stories of Victoria's Multicultural Past*. Victoria: TouchWood Editions, 2018.

Stella Carroll

Dunae, Patrick. "Geographies of sexual commerce and the production of prostitutional space: Victoria, British Columbia, 1860–1914." *Journal of the Canadian Historical Association*, vol. 19, no.1, 2008. Accessed March 25, 2020. https://www.cliomedia.ca/articles/dunae_geographies.pdf.

Eversole, Linda, J. *Stella: Unrepentant Madam*. Victoria: TouchWood Editions, 2005.

Hanson-Brett, C.L. "Ladies in Scarlet: An Historical Overview of Prostitution in Victoria, British Columbia 1870–1939." *British Columbia Historical News*, vol. 19, no. 2, 1986: 21–24. Accessed on March 26, 2020. http://www.library.ubc.ca/archives/pdfs/bchf/bchn_1986_01.pdf.

Hawthorn, Tom. "Victoria's Colourful History of Sex for Sale." *The Globe and Mail*, October 26, 2010. https://www.theglobeandmail.com/news/british-columbia/victorias-colourful-history-of-sex-for-sale/article4330710/.

Kersey, Bill. "Victoria's Glory Years." *Victoria Daily Colonist*, April 23, 1978.

Ruttan, Stephen. "Stella: When Only the Best Will Do." *Times Colonist*, October 28, 2012.

Watts, Richard. "UVic Condo Plan for Old Town Site Irks Victoria Councillor." *Western Investor*, July 4, 2018. Accessed November 25, 2018. https://www.westerninvestor.com/news/british-columbia/uvic-condo-plan-for-old-town-site-irks-victoria-councillor-1.23357630.

Josette Legacé Work

Adams, John. "Hillside-Quadra." 2019. Victoria Heritage Foundation website. Accessed March 24, 2020. https://victoriaheritagefoundation.ca/Neighbourhoods/hillside quadrahistory.html.

Douglas, Brodie. "Métis Nation of British Columbia: BC Métis History." Accessed March 24, 2020. https://www.mnbc.ca/about/metis-history.

Gould, Jan. *Women of British Columbia*. Surrey: Hancock House Publishers, 1975.

Facing History and Ourselves. "Métis." Accessed March 24, 2020. https://www.facing history.org/stolen-lives-indigenous-peoples-canada-and-indian-residential-schools/historical-background/m-tis.

Fort Nisqually Living History Museum. "Person Record: Work, Josette Legacé." Accessed March 24, 2020. https://fortnisqually.pastperfectonline.com/byperson?keyword=Work%2C+Josette+Legace.

Hudson's Bay Company History Foundation. "Life of a Voyageur." Accessed March 24, 2020. http://www.hbcheritage.ca/classroom/virtual-museum/fur-trade-nation/life-of-a-voyageur.

Maloney, Alice. "John Work of the Hudson's Bay Company: Leader of the California Brigade of 1832–33." *California Historical Society Quarterly*, vol. 22, issue 2 (June 1943): 97–107. https://doi.org/10.2307/25155777.

McIlroy, Anne. "Canada's Forgotten People." *The Guardian*, September 23, 2003. Accessed on March 24, 2020. https://www.theguardian.com/world/2003/sep/23/worlddispatch.annemcilroy.

Van Kirk, Sylvia. "Legace, Josette." *Dictionary of Canadian Biography*, vol. 12 (2003). Accessed March 24, 2020. http://www.biographi.ca/en/bio/legace_josette_12E.html.

Wong, May Q. *City in Colour: Rediscovered Stories of Victoria's Multicultural Past*. Victoria: TouchWood Editions, 2018.

Jennie Butchart

Artibise, Alan. "Saanich Peninsula." *The Canadian Encyclopedia*, February 7, 2006. Accessed on March 23, 2020. https://www.thecanadianencyclopedia.ca/en/article/saanich-peninsula.

Birds of a Feather: Victoria B & B. "Butchart Family History—Robert and Jennie."
Accessed March 21, 2020. https://www.birdsofafeather.ca/butchart-family-history.

Canada's Historic Places. "Butchart Gardens National Historic Site of Canada."
Accessed March 21, 2020. https://www.historicplaces.ca/en/rep-reg/place-lieu.
aspx?id=7821&pid=0.

Forbes, Elizabeth. "Beauty of the Gardens Brings Founders Close." *Victoria Daily Times*, August 5, 1960.

Forster, Merna. *100 More Canadian Heroines: Famous and Forgotten Faces*. Toronto:
Dundurn Press, 2004.

McLeod. Susanna. "Canada Ingenuity: Colour, Life Where None Existed." *The Kingston Whig Standard*, March 31, 2015. https://www.thewhig.com/2015/03/31/canadian-ingenuity-colour-life-where-none-existed/wcm/042ef319-b342-a762-1440-1811bfd6c331.

Preston, Dave. *The Story of Butchart Gardens*. Victoria: Highline Publishing, 1996.

Reynolds, Mac. "Mrs. Butchart's Famous Gardens." *Maclean's Magazine*, September 15, 1952. https://archive.macleans.ca/article/1952/9/15/mrs-butcharts-famous-gardens.

Times Colonist. "Daughters Inherit $500 000 in Estate of Mrs. Butchart," May 19, 1951.

——. "Mrs. R.P. Butchart," December 14, 1950.

——. "Scatter Mrs. Butchart's Ashes on Inlet Waters," December 14, 1950.

The Butchart Gardens. "Our Story," 2020. Accessed March 21, 2020. https://www.
butchartgardens.com/our-story/.

Walton, Avis. "Famed Garden was Vision of Jenny Butchart." *Daily Colonist*, July 21, 1945.

Vancouver Sun. "Creator of Famed Island Garden Dies," December 14, 1950.

Wolf, Jim. "Isaburo Kishida: British Columbia Pioneer Japanese Landscape Designer.".
Sitelines: British Columbia Society of Landscape Architects, February 2003.
Accessed March 23, 2020. http://www.urbanecology.ca/documents/Journal%20
Articles/Sitelines2003.pdf.

Minnie Paterson

Forbes, Elizabeth. *Wild Roses at Their Feet: Pioneer Women of Vancouver Island*.
Vancouver: Evergreen Press Ltd., 1971.

Gill, Ian, and David Nanuk (photog.). *Hiking on the Edge: West Coast Trail, Juan de Fuca Trail*. Vancouver: Raincoast Books, 1998.

Graham, Donald. *Keepers of the Light: A History of British Columbia's Lighthouses and Their Keepers*. Madiera Park, BC: Harbour Publishing, 1985.

Green, Valerie, and Lynn Gordon-Findlay (illust.). *If More Walls Could Talk: Vancouver Island's Houses from the Past*. Victoria: TouchWood Editions, 2004.

Mason, Adrienne. *West Coast Adventures: Shipwrecks, Lighthouses, and Rescues Along Canada's West Coast*. Canmore, AB: Altitude Publishing Canada Ltd, 2003.

Peterson, Jan. *The Albernis, 1860–1922*. Victoria: Oolichan Books, 1992.
Paterson, T. W. "Minnie Paterson Braved Storm to Fetch Rescuers for *Coloma*." *Daily Colonist*, November 20, 1906.

Maria Mahoi

Barman, Jean. "Mahoi (Mahoy, Magoi), Maria." *Dictionary of Canadian Biography*, vol. 16 (2003). Accessed March 15, 2020. http://www.biographi.ca/en/bio/mahoi_maria_16E.html.
———. *Maria Mahoi of the Islands*. Vancouver: New Star Books, 2017.
Parks Canada. "Hawaiian Settlement on Russell Island." Accessed March 7, 2020. https://www.pc.gc.ca/en/pn-np/bc/gulf/culture/hawaienne-hawaiian.
Wong, May Q. *City in Colour: Rediscovered Stories of Victoria's Multicultural Past*. Victoria: TouchWood Editions, 2018.

Sylvia Stark

Great Unsolved Mysteries in Canadian History. "Louis and Sylvia Stark," *Who Killed William Robinson: Race, Justice and Settling the Land*. Accessed July 27, 2019. https://www.canadianmysteries.ca/sites/robinson/murder/castofcharacters/1720en.html.
Gulf Islands Driftwood. "B.C. Spells Freedom for the Estes, Starks," December 12, 1979.
Hamilton, Bea. *Salt Spring Island*. Vancouver: Mitchell Press Limited, 1969.
Kahn, Charles. *Salt Spring: The Story of an Island*. Madiera Park, BC: Harbour Publishing, 1998.
Nanaimo Free Press. "Mrs. Stark, 106, Salt Spring Island, Ex-Slave, Passes-on," October 1944.
The Daily Colonist. "Story Recalls Tough Life of Island Black Pioneers." June 26, 1974.
Nanaimo Free Press. "Died—Louis Stark." February 28, 1895.
Poirier, Genevre. "Stark Family Landed During Black History Month." *Star*, March 1, 2006.
Royal British Columbia Museum and Archives. "Sylvia Estes Stark." Accessed January 30, 2020. https://royalbcmuseum.bc.ca/exhibits/bc-archives-time-machine/galler10/frames/stark.htm.
Salt Spring Island Archives. "Estes/Stark Family." Accessed July 27, 2019. http://saltspringarchives.com/Naidine/index.htm.
Salt Spring Island Historical Society. "Amazing Women of Salt Spring Island," 2008. Accessed August 14, 2019. saltspringarchives.com/women.pdf.
Stark-Wallace, Marie. "From Slavery to Freedom: The History of the Stark Family." *Gulf Islands Driftwood* (Salt Spring Island, BC). Ten-part series, 1979.

Veronica Milner

Austin, Alfred. *In Veronica's Garden*. London: Macmillan and Co., 1895.
Cadwaladr, Margaret. *In Veronica's Garden*. Royston, BC: Madrona Books and Publishing, 2002.

Bibliography and References

Cooper, Lucy. *The Element Encyclopedia Of Fairies: An A-Z of Fairies, Pixies and other Fantastical Creatures.* London: Harper Element, 2014.

Vancouver Island University. "Milner Story: Background of Milner Gardens & Woodland." Accessed June 23, 2019. https://www2.viu.ca/milnergardens/history.asp.

Barbara Touchie (Sičquuʔuƛ)

First Voices. "Nuu-chah-nulth (Barkley) Home Page." Accessed March 8, 2020. http://legacy.firstvoices.com/en/Nuu-chah-nulth/word/2a99bca938427ebc/working

Maffi, Luisa. "Learning Our Language is Like Learning to See in Full Color: An Interview with Gisèle Maria Martin (Tla-o-qui-aht)." *Landscape Magazine,* November 6, 2019. https://medium.com/langscape-magazine/learning-our-language-is-like-learning-to-see-in-full-color-an-interview-with-gisele-maria-martin-fd497ebf86a1.

Mundy, Vi. Personal interview, February 28, 2020.

O'Malley, Nora. "Pacific Rim National Park Honours Barbara Touchie." *Tofino-Ucluelet Westerly News,* Oct 13, 2016. https://www.westerlynews.ca/community/pacific-rim-national-park-honours-barbara-touchie/.

Parks Canada. "Barbara Touchie (1931–2014)." Accessed March 8, 2020. https://www.canada.ca/en/parks-canada/news/2016/09/barbara-touchie-1931-2014.html

Parks Canada. "Pacific Rim National Park Reserve: Kwisitis Visitor Centre." Accessed March 8, 2020. https://www.pc.gc.ca/en/pn-np/bc/pacificrim/activ/activkwisitis.

Edith Berkeley

Ainley, Marianne. "Berkeley [formerly Bergtheil; née Dunington], Edith (1875–1963)." *Oxford Dictionary of National Biography.* Accessed June 23, 2019. https://www.oxforddnb.com/view/10.1093/ref:odnb/9780198614128.001.0001/odnb-9780198614128-e-59328;jsessionid=30B24DC7A2ED9A353B7B7E46F22A5138.

———. *Despite the Odds: Essays on Canadian Women and Science.* Montreal: Véhicule Press, 1990.

Canadian Aquatic Resources Section of the American Fisheries Society. "Legends of Canadian Fisheries, Science and Management." Accessed June 23, 2019. https://cars.fisheries.org/legends-of-canadian-fisheries-science-and-management/#Edith%20Berkeley.

Holmlund, Mona, & Youngberg, Gail. *Inspiring Women: A Celebration of Herstory.* Regina, SK: Coteau Books, 2003.

Hubbard, J. M., Wildish, D., & Stephenson, R. *A Century of Marine Science: The St. Andrews Biological Station.* Toronto: University of Toronto Press, 2016.

Knowbc.com. "Berkeley's Eualid." Accessed June 23, 2019. http://knowbc.com/books/
    Marine-Life-of-the-Pacific-Northwest/Invertebrates/Arthropods/Shrimps/
    AR56-BERKELEYS-EUALID.
Needler, A. "Edith and Cyril Berkeley." *Canadian Encyclopedia*, April 13, 2018.
    Accessed June 23, 2019. https://www.thecanadianencyclopedia.ca/en/article/
    edith-and-cyril-berkeley.
Pettibone, M. H. "Specimens of Polychaetes Described by Edith and Cyril Berkeley
    (1923-1964)," *Proceedings of the United States National Museum*, 119(3553),
    Smithsonian Institution, Washington, DC, 1967. Accessed June 23, 2019. https://
    repository.si.edu/bitstream/handle/10088/16987/USNMP-119_3553_1967.
    pdf?sequence=1&isAllowed=y.
Purcell, J. E., & Welch, D. W. "In Memoriam: Dr. Mary N. Arai." *PICES Press*, 26(2),
    2018, pp. 15-16. Accessed June 23, 2019. http://meetings.pices.int/publications/
    pices-press/volume26/PPJul2018.pdf.
Redford, Gabrielle. "WhyShould We Care about Marine Worms?" *National Wildlife
    Federation*, April 1, 2001. Accessed June 23, 2019. https://www.nwf.org/en/
    Magazines/National-Wildlife/2001/Marine-Worms.

Mary Ellen Smith

Bellett, Gerry. "B.C. Heroes: Mary Ellen Smith." *Vancouver Sun*, March 3, 2011.
Fair Vote Canada. "Proportional Representation." Accessed March 20, 2020. https://
    www.fairvote.ca/proportional-representation/.
Forbes, Elizabeth. "Mary Ellen Was First to Serve." *Victoria Daily Times*, February 4, 1966.
Legislative Assembly of British Columbia. "Mary Ellen Smith." Accessed March 19,
    2020. https://www.leg.bc.ca/wotv/pages/featured-women/mary-ellen-smith.aspx.
Matthews, Meryl. "Mary Ellen Led Way in Politics." *Kamloops Daily Sentinel*, February 14, 1975.
Morton, James. "Ralph and Mary Ellen Smith Notable in Public Life." *Times Colonist*,
    February 21, 1951.
Nesbitt, James. "A History of Portfolios and Petticoats." *Vancouver Sun*, January 26, 1980.
——. "Amor De Cosmos." *Vancouver Sun*, January 27, 1967.
——. "Mary Ellen Smith." *Vancouver Sun*, November 22, 1969.
Peterson, Jan. *Harbour City: Nanaimo in Transition, 1920–1967*. Victoria: Heritage
    House Publishing, 2006.
Strong-Boag, Veronica. "Precedents for Today's 'Big Tent' Liberalism: British
    Columbia's First Woman MLA, Mary Ellen Spear Smith (1863–1933)," Active
    History: University of Saskatchewan and Huron University College, February 2,
    2018. http://activehistory.ca/2018/02/precedents-for-todays-big-tent-liberalism-
    british-columbias-first-woman-mla-mary-ellen-spear-smith-1863-1933/.

Pansy May Stuttard

Bremner, Maria I. *Cape Scott and the North Coast Trail: Hiking Vancouver Island's Wildest Coast.* Madeira Park, BC: Harbour Publishing, 2015.

Cullen, Gary. "Delta residents share their memories to mark Canada's 150th birthday." *Surrey Now-Leader,* October 28, 2017. https://www.surreynowleader.com/community/delta-residents-share-their-memories-to-mark-canadas-150th-birthday.

Geni. "Pansy May Stuttard." Accessed August 10, 2019. https://www.geni.com/people/Pansy-May-Stuttard/6000000089354904883.

Ladner Optimist. "Colorful Character of S. Delta Died May 23," June 5, 1963.

———. "First Coastal Woman Master Doesn't Regret," July 19, 1951.

Northern Vancouver Island: The Undiscovered Coast. "Sea Otter Cove: Historical Photo of the Week" (blog entry), February 10, 2017. http://undiscoveredcoast.blogspot.com/2017/02/sea-otter-cove-historical-photo-of-week.html

Russwurm, Lani. "Vancouver Was Awesome: Pansy May Stuttard, 1958." *Vancouver Is Awesome,* January 1, 2014. Accessed June 12, 2019. https://www.vancouverisawesome.com/history/vancouver-was-awesome-pansy-may-stuttard-1958-1928078.

Vancouver Sun. "84-Year-Old Woman Robbed by Bandit Gang in Surrey," December 31, 1957.

Archives

Alberni District Historical Society, Port Alberni

City of Victoria Archives, Victoria

Nanaimo Community Archives, Nanaimo

Royal British Columbia Museum and Archives, Victoria

Salt Spring Island Archives, Ganges

University Archives and Special Collections, University of Saskatchewan, Saskatoon

Acknowledgements

MANY THANKS TO Heritage House Publishing and Lara Kordic for supporting the telling of these stories and for another opportunity to write about trailblazing women of Vancouver Island. Special thanks to editor Nandini Thaker, whose edits and insights made this book infinitely better.

Thank you to Vi Mundy, daughter of Barbara Touchie, who greatly helped with Barbara Touchie's story, but also deeply inspired me. Thank you to The Butchart Gardens; Joy Bremner at Mid Island Métis Nation; Jan Ovans at Cowichan Valley Métis Nation; Lea Edgar at the Vancouver Maritime Museum; Blair Galson at the Pacific Mountain Region United Church of Canada; Darryl MacKenzie at the City of Delta and the Delta Heritage Society; Sarah Rathjen at the City of Victoria Archives; Ceridwen Ross Collins at the Salt Spring Archives; Kristen Smith at the Alberni Valley Museum; Kelly-Ann Turkington at the BC Archives, Kristin Wenberg for the author photo; and Vicki Nygaard, Chair and Professor of Studies in Women and Gender at Vancouver Island University.

Thank you to my parents, Michael and Cathy Kuntz; my sisters, Carmen Kuntz and Alison Martin; and the Healey family. Lastly, thank you to Steven Healey for the limitless support with this book and everything.

Index